30-SECOND
LONDON

30-SECOND
LONDON

The 50 key visions, events and architects that shaped the city, each explained in half a minute

Editor
Edward Denison

Contributors
Nick Beech
Edward Denison
Emily Gee
Simon Inglis
Alan Powers
Matthew Shaw
Jane Sidell

Illustrations
Nicky Ackland-Snow

IVY PRESS

First published in the UK in 2017 by

Ivy Press
Ovest House
58 West Street
Brighton BN1 2RA
United Kingdom
www.quartoknows.com

British Library Cataloguing-in-
Publication Data
A catalogue record for this
book is available from the
British Library.

ISBN: 978-1-78240-454-5

This book was conceived,
designed and produced by

Ivy Press

Publisher **Susan Kelly**
Creative Director **Michael Whitehead**
Editorial Director **Tom Kitch**
Art Director **Wayne Blades**
Commissioning Editor **Sophie Collins**
Project Editor **Joanna Bentley**
Designer **Ginny Zeal**
Picture Researcher **Katie Greenwood**

Typeset in Section

Printed in China

10 9 8 7 6 5 4 3 2 1

CONTENTS

INTRODUCTION

Edward Denison

London is an extraordinary city. No other modern metropolis possesses such a long and continuous history, the evidence of which can be read in its streets and buildings, its governance and institutions, its commerce and culture. From its Roman origins early in the first millennia to its global eminence at the dawn of the third millennia, London's success has relied on exchange – of goods and of ideas. This exchange has been conducted by countless people within and far beyond the city's borders, the accumulation of which has created a historical record that fills more shelf space than any other city on earth. History weighs heavily on London, but it is also the source of its inspiration and constant renewal. This book has been conceived and written in response to this fragile relationship between the enduring and the ephemeral that has simultaneously built on the city's past, avoided its stagnation and stimulated its growth. This delicate balancing act is London's story – a resilient tale of tragedy and triumph spanning two thousand years.

London is many things to many people. Ask any commuter who has to endure the daily slog to and from work and they will complain bitterly, yet they will measure their suburban idyll by its proximity in minutes from the city centre. Ask a student and they will bemoan the cost of living, yet spend freely in the city's bars and clubs. Ask a City banker or trader and they will claim to be the city's lifeblood, while wilfully bleeding it dry. Ask an architect and they will whine about the city's appearance, yet be desperate to add their signature to the chaos. Don't even ask a city planner, they don't appear to be from this planet! Ask a tourist and they will worship its history, yet denounce the antiquated accommodation and outmoded Tube. Ask a refugee and they will be grateful for the city's sanctuary, unaware of the historical precedent in their journey. Ask a resident and they will delight in complaining while quietly appreciating being able to call this alluring, exhilarating, enriching, impossible, uncontrollable, quaint, welcoming and wonderful city home.

History inspires London, from the neo-Gothic Elizabeth Tower that houses Big Ben to the Shard (2013), which recalls London's church spires and the tower of nearby Southwark Cathedral.

Of all the views depicted of London and opinions expressed over the centuries, the most famous was by Samuel Johnson, who, in 1777, wrote: 'when a man is tired of London, he is tired of life; for there is in London all that life can afford'. It is fitting that such a truism was quoted by someone who would not consider themselves a Londoner, but then what is a Londoner? London is too large and too complex to offer itself to any individual. Its appeal is its inscrutability – anyone can make London their home and feel at home, and millions do.

How this book works

This book has been written by scholars who live and work in London and for whom London is a central theme in their work, whether through teaching or research. The purpose of the book is to illuminate London's past so as to make sense of the present. **Birth of the City** deals with origins, the earth on which the city was built, those who have made it their home, and the constellation of settlements that helped define its polycentric character. The second chapter, **Building London**, looks at those who legislated and financed its growth, and the form its major developments took, from planned streets and squares to sprawling suburbs. We then look at the city's assorted **Architecture**, from the advent of the profession to the latest glass and steel erections. Chapter four, **Arts & Culture**, focuses on London's creative spirit, acknowledging its contribution to creative inspiration and cultural resistance. **Innovation & Learning** looks into London's world-class museums, galleries and educational institutions, marvelling at some of the practical outputs of this knowledge in the feats of engineering that have allowed the city to grow and its population to thrive. **Business & Pleasure** observes what makes London tick – the places and spaces where Londoners do business and find pleasure. Finally, **Enigmatic London** discovers the city's quirkier characteristics and reveals its dark side.

The magnificent roof covering the Queen Elizabeth II Great Court inside the British Museum, redesigned by Foster and Partners (2000).

pre-1000

43 CE
Romans invade Britain

50
Founding of Londinium

60
Boudica leads a rebellion against the Romans and destroys Londinium

886
King Alfred establishes Lundenburh within the old Roman walls

1300s

1348–9
The Black Death kills half London's population

1381
Peasants' Revolt, an anti-taxation protest

1500s

1538–40
Dissolution of the monasteries closes many abbeys and priories in London and elsewhere

1599
The Globe theatre opens

1600s

1616
Queen's House, London's first classical building, is designed by Inigo Jones

1665
The Great Plague kills about 100,000 people in London

1666
Great Fire of London

Each entry is made up of a 30-second tour which explores the subject, the essence of which is distilled into a 3-second survey. A further 3-minute overview elaborates on the topic by concentrating on a specific detail. A biographic spread in each chapter illuminates an individual associated with the overarching theme of the chapter.

1700s

1710
St Paul's Cathedral, designed by Christopher Wren, is completed

1750
Completion of Westminster Bridge, London's first 'modern' bridge

1759
Opening of the British Museum

1780
Gordon Riots, an anti-Catholic protest

1800s

1829
Founding of the Metropolitan Police

1851
The Great Exhibition held in the Crystal Palace

1863
Opening of the Underground

1870
Building of the Houses of Parliament at Westminster completed

1900s

1940–41
The Blitz, intensive bombing of London by the German Luftwaffe

1951
Festival of Britain on the South Bank

1976
Opening of the Museum of London

1990
Poll tax riots against local taxation changes

2000s

2000
Millennium celebrations marked by major projects including the Dome, Bridge and Wheel (London Eye)

BIRTH OF THE CITY

BIRTH OF THE CITY
GLOSSARY

Aldermen of the Wards Officers elected every six years to the Court of Aldermen from each of the 25 Wards that constitute the City of London.

Aliens Act, 1905 An Act of Parliament imposing immigration controls into Britain for the first time.

City of London A city and county of Britain governed by the City of London Corporation covering a geographic area broadly defined by the walls of the Roman settlement, also referred to as the Square Mile.

cretaceous Geological period from 145.5–65.5 million years ago that marked the last epoch in the age of the dinosaurs.

Dissolution of the Monasteries, 1536–40 The seizure of all monastic lands and property by Henry VIII following the Reformation, when the Church of England split from the Roman Catholic Church.

drift geology Glacial materials, including sand and rocks, deposited on land or at sea.

Greater London Metropolitan area of London comprising 32 boroughs and the City of London, administered by the Greater London Authority (GLA).

Hanseatic League Organization based in northern Europe established to promote and protect commercial interests and merchant guilds in the Baltic region from the fourteenth to eighteenth centuries.

Huguenot French Protestant movement established in the sixteenth century and subjected to state-sponsored persecution, causing tens of thousands to flee to England in the seventeenth century.

Iceni Tribe occupying territory in East Anglia (Norfolk and Suffolk) from the Iron Age to the Roman invasion (43 CE).

livery companies Trade and craft associations based in the City of London also known as guilds, whose name derives from the uniforms that distinguished one livery company from another.

Lord Mayor of London The head of the City of London Corporation elected annually and not to be confused with the Mayor of London, the head of the Greater London Authority.

river pageant Flotilla of boats, often including the royal barge, held on the River Thames to celebrate or commemorate important state occasions.

solid geology The geology of solid material such as bedrock, often covered by the accumulation of drift and top soil.

tea clippers Very fast sailing ships designed to bring back fresh produce, especially tea, from Asia during the nineteenth century, before the advent of motorized shipping.

GEOLOGY & GEOGRAPHY

the 30-second tour

London is situated in a

cretaceous chalk basin and is surrounded by chalk hills – the Chilterns, the Berkshire Downs and the North Downs. The chalk is covered with marine sands, gravels and clay (forming the solid geology), dating from approximately 60 million years ago when Britain was submerged. Fluctuations in the sea level mean London was physically part of the European landmass for significantly longer than it has been separated. The basin is bisected north–south by the River Thames, which was dramatically shoved into this location by a glacier nearly half a million years ago, with a series of tributary rivers such as the Fleet and Lea draining into it. This event changed London forever as the river drew early humans to fresh water and food. During the ice ages, the advance and retreat of ice sheets moved gravel into the Thames, subsequently deposited as river terraces, forming a staircase dropping down to the current floodplain. These gravels form the drift geology, which in some areas is capped by silts blown off the ice sheets, known as loess or brickearth. In these terraces, flint tools, bones and plants have been found and studied since the seventeenth century, documenting how humans and animals have lived by the Thames for nearly half a million years in freezing tundra, hot grasslands, dense forests and marshes.

3-SECOND SURVEY
The geology and geographical position of London were key to its beginnings as a human settlement.

3-MINUTE OVERVIEW
Over the last 440,000 years, London has produced evidence for the most exotic fauna in Britain. During the cold stages, Neanderthals jostled with woolly mammoth and rhino, cave bears, wolves and giant deer. Trafalgar Square has provided the best British evidence for the last warm stage, 100,000 years ago, when elephants, lions and hippos roamed through a savannah beside the Thames.

RELATED TOPIC
See also
THE THAMES
page 22

3-SECOND BIOGRAPHY
JOHN CONYERS
1633–94
London antiquarian, the first person to recognize flint tools as made rather than natural objects

30-SECOND TEXT
Jane Sidell

Archaeology has unearthed some amazing discoveries in London, such as evidence of elephants, lions and hippos from 100,000 years ago.

ROMAN LONDON

the 30-second tour

In 43 CE the Romans, led by Emperor Claudius, invaded Britain and built the city of Londinium on two hills beside the Thames. Initially it was formed of wooden buildings, gravel streets and a military encampment, all of which was destroyed by Queen Boudica in 60 CE. However, the city was rapidly rebuilt and became the provincial capital. Expansive development included an amphitheatre, fort, temples, townhouses and public baths. Trade thrived as wine, spices and pottery were imported from Rome, Syria and Egypt while exports included tin, jet and slaves. Around 200 CE, the 3-kilometre-long (9-mile) town wall was built; standing over 6 metres (20 feet) high, it enclosed roughly the same area as the modern City of London. Outside the wall, cemeteries lined the roads to other towns. At its height, it is estimated that 30,000 people lived in Londinium. Originating from Britain, France and other Roman provinces, they all spoke Latin as the common tongue. Evidence survives for a variety of customs, including worship of Celtic, Classical and Eastern gods, including Isis, Mars, Mithras, and the Emperor himself. In 410 CE the Emperor Honorius abandoned Britain, and Londinium's population declined. Buildings collapsed and the area was not reoccupied until King Alfred created Lundenburh in 886 CE.

3-SECOND SURVEY
What did the Romans ever do for London? Gave us wine, roads, writing, temples, a bridge, a name and a capital city.

3-MINUTE OVERVIEW
Much of Londinium has been destroyed, or is deeply buried, but traces do survive. Part of the amphitheatre can be seen in the Guildhall Art Gallery, while sections of the City Wall still stand, with the best at St Alphege Garden, Coopers Row and Tower Hill. Thousands of Roman objects are displayed in the Museum of London, with mosaics alongside sculptures, wine jars, jewellery and shoes, down to tiny coins and earrings.

RELATED TOPIC
See also
BOUDICA
page 20

3-SECOND BIOGRAPHY
TIBERIUS CLAUDIUS DRUSUS NERO GERMANICUS
10 BCE–54 CE
Became Emperor in 41 CE following the assassination of his nephew Caligula. In addition to conquering Britain, he oversaw successful invasions in North Africa and Turkey. He was poisoned by his wife, Agrippina

30-SECOND TEXT
Jane Sidell

London was founded by the Romans soon after their invasion in 43 CE under Emperor Claudius, who went on to invade much of North Africa.

43 CE
Roman invasion of
Britain. Boudica is
probably a child at
this time

47–48
The Iceni tribe rebel
unsuccessfully against
Roman rule

59
Boudica's husband
Prasutagus dies. His land
is seized by the Romans

60–61
Boudica leads a major
rebellion, destroying
Colchester, London and
St Albans, but is defeated
at an unknown battlefield
and dies, possibly by
poisoning herself

BOUDICA

Boudica is the earliest

documented woman in British history.
She was an Iron Age leader who led a significant
rebellion against Rome in 60 or 61 CE, and very
nearly won. Boudica has become an enduring
legend, her story hijacked for propaganda,
portrayed as noble patriot, cruel barbarian,
grieving mother, dangerously sensual savage
and feminist icon. Plays, poems and pamphlets
have been written about her from an early
age, a dignity afforded to remarkably few
British women.

The first writers to acknowledge Boudica
were the classical authors Tacitus and Dio;
Tacitus wrote within living memory, while Dio
over a hundred years later. Nothing is known
of her early life. She enters history as wife to
Prasutagus, leader of the Iceni tribe of East
Anglia. His correct title is uncertain, but
Boudica will forever be a Warrior Queen in
popular literature. Dio described her as tall,
terrifying and harsh-sounding with red hair
cascading to her hips.

When Prasutagus died in 59 CE, the Romans
violently annexed his territory, flogged Boudica
and raped her daughters. She raised an army
and marched on Camulodunum (Colchester),
which was then a colony of Roman army
veterans, and sacked the settlement. Boudica
then headed to London, which Tacitus states
was 'not a settlement' (a planned city) but was
important for trade. With only limited troops,
the Provincial Governor Suetonius abandoned
London, which was razed to the ground by
Boudica's army. Extensive archaeological
evidence exists for the fire here and also at
Verulamium (St Albans) where Boudica turned
next. She was finally defeated by Suetonius
at an unidentified battlefield in the Midlands.
Tacitus suggests 80,000 Britons died in this
battle, against 400 Roman deaths. He also
describes the extreme violence meted out by
Boudica on Roman soldiers and civilians.

Dio claims Boudica became ill, died and
received an elaborate burial, whereas Tacitus
writes that she took poison, presumably to
avoid the ritual humiliation often inflicted by
the Romans. Her remains have never been
found, although many myths perpetuate,
most famously that she is buried under King's
Cross railway station. Her destruction of
London may have accelerated its development
from small trading centre to provincial capital,
by prompting rapid development and strong
town planning. Furthermore, her destruction
of Colchester and St Albans left a need for a
Roman power base, for which London was
geographically well suited.

Historical accounts and images of Boudica
have been used to portray classical superiority
over barbarians, and the unnaturalness and
danger when women step outside traditional
gender roles.

Jane Sidell

THE THAMES

the 30-second tour

The River Thames gets its name

from the Celtic *Tamesis*, as used by Julius Caesar in his *Histories*. The 380-kilometre-long (235-mile) river rises in the Cotswolds, flows west to east, before meeting the North Sea, with a 90-kilometre (55-mile) tidal stretch. It has carved a wide valley for over 440,000 years, but was only bridged in the first century CE by the Romans near modern-day London Bridge, then again in 1209. The city currently has 34 bridges, the majority constructed in the nineteenth century. London's first exclusively pedestrian bridge, the Millennium Bridge, was opened in 2000. Several tunnels pass beneath the Thames, most famously that constructed by Marc and Isambard Kingdom Brunel at Rotherhithe, where they developed the tunnelling shield to excavate safely in unstable ground. The Thames has been a port and transport hub for nearly 2,000 years, with Romans trading across the Empire, a Saxon beach market on the Strand, medieval merchants striking deals on the City waterfront and Tudor explorers setting out to conquer the New World. The river is administered by the Environment Agency and Port of London Authority, who oversee many activities, from freight traffic to river pageants, and even the arcane tradition of swan upping, the annual audit of Thames swans.

3-SECOND SURVEY
Playing a vital role in transport, business and culture, the River Thames has been central to London's development.

3-MINUTE OVERVIEW
The Thames River Police, established in 1798, is the oldest police force in the world. It was formed to protect life and goods by curbing the rampant crime that pervaded the river, docks, and warehouses. Theft, assault, smuggling and indeed piracy existed on the Thames for centuries, even amongst the aristocracy, including Sir Francis Drake. Many pirates sailed from the Thames and ended their days at Execution Dock, most famously Captain Kidd.

RELATED TOPICS
See also
GEOLOGY & GEOGRAPHY
page 16

MARITIME LONDON & EMPIRE
page 26

ENGINEERING
page 106

LOST RIVERS
page 150

3-SECOND BIOGRAPHIES
SIR FRANCIS DRAKE
c. 1540–96
Explorer, mariner and pirate

CAPTAIN WILLIAM KIDD
1645–1701
Legendary pirate of the Caribbean

ISAMBARD KINGDOM BRUNEL
1806–59
Britain's greatest engineer, responsible for bridges, ships, tunnels and railway networks

30-SECOND TEXT
Jane Sidell

The River Thames has defined London's development, as well as providing a home to diverse flora and fauna.

TWO CITIES
the 30-second tour

When the historian John Stow
set out in 1598 to survey London he could walk
across and comprehend it within an afternoon.
London was still a medieval city – bounded by
ancient walls, towers and gates, and thick with
low buildings and narrow streets. The skyline
was dominated by church spires, the Tower in
the east, and St Paul's in the west. Noisy, smelly
and crowded (200,000 people in Stow's time),
London was alive by day and dark by night.
The city was a centre of commerce and language
(cried out and printed), ruled by the Lord
Mayor and Aldermen of the Wards, elected
by members of the livery companies who
controlled craft and trade. A mile to the west
lay the City of Westminster, dominated by
the Palaces of Whitehall and St James's and the
great St Peter's Church of Westminster Abbey.
Westminster was the city of the Crown and
state. Connecting London and Westminster was
the Strand, hugging the banks of the Thames
and strung with villas and palaces of courtiers.
Outside these two Cities, beyond the jurisdiction
of the Lord Mayor or the Crown, new districts
full of theatres, bear-baiting pits, brothels and
the houses of bishops were emerging, hinting
at London's future growth. These included
Southwark, on the south bank of the river, and
Spitalfields, beyond the Tower to the east.

3-SECOND SURVEY
Greater London includes
two cities (London and
Westminster), completely
different in character, still
observable today with
different governments,
policing arrangements
and even street furniture.

3-MINUTE OVERVIEW
The City of London is
older than the nation in
which it is situated. Its
institutions – Lord Mayor,
Aldermen and liveries –
have been maintained in
parallel with the Crown.
The Corporation of London
has responsibility for the
City, and has never been
absorbed into the wider
government of 'Greater
London'. Though the wall
surrounding the City has
long gone, the boundary
is clearly marked by iron
dragons, derived from
London's Coat of Arms.

RELATED TOPICS
See also
VILLAGES
page 28

THE EAST & WEST ENDS
page 36

MAPPING LONDON
page 152

3-SECOND BIOGRAPHIES
JOHN STOW
c. 1525–1605
Antiquarian admitted to
the freedom of the Merchant
Taylors Company in 1547,
who completed his *Survey
of London* in 1598

JOHN STRYPE
1643–1737
Clergyman and antiquarian.
A Huguenot silk merchant and
throwster, Strype updated
Stow's *Survey* in 1720,
recording the very many
transformations of London

30-SECOND TEXT
Nick Beech

*Westminster and
the City are both
dominated by their
religious structures
dedicated to St Peter
and St Paul espectively.*

MARITIME LONDON & EMPIRE

the 30-second tour

3-SECOND SURVEY

London's docks have sent ships all over the world for trade, war and empire-building.

3-MINUTE OVERVIEW

Whale hunting was a key aspect of the port economy from the early seventeenth century, with blubber turned into oil to provide light. A fleet was established hunting bowhead whales in the Arctic, then expanded everywhere, including the Pacific, where the London-based South Sea Company was the first to hunt. The height of the trade was in the late eighteenth century when the fleet comprised dozens of ships sailing from the Greenland Dock, hunting thousands of whales.

Since the Roman period, the port of London has been integral to international trade. In the twelfth century the Hanseatic League established a trading base in London; subsequently many merchant companies were founded to trade and raise revenue for the government. The East India Company, founded in 1600 and still operating today, was particularly famous for trading spices in Asia. Merchants traded from the kilometres of wharves lining the Thames, which became so crowded with vessels that artificial docks were dug from the seventeenth century to increase capacity, including the Blackwall and West India Docks. Military bases were constructed downstream to build ships and weapons for the Navy, including Deptford Dockyard and Woolwich Arsenal. Ship-breaking also took place on the foreshore, where unseaworthy vessels were stripped down. The merchant fleet traded all around the world and as the British Empire grew in the eighteenth and nineteenth centuries, the importance of the port of London – the heart of Empire – grew with it. Ships carried goods, but also the people of Empire – administrators, colonists, the military, artists, wives, aspiring wives and criminals. The *Cutty Sark* tea clipper, now in permanent dry dock at Greenwich, is one of the finest surviving elements of maritime London.

RELATED TOPIC

See also
THE THAMES
page 22

3-SECOND BIOGRAPHY

JOHN HAWKINS
1532–95
Merchant adventurer, trader, privateer, spy and slaver. Rear Admiral of the fleet fighting the Spanish Armada

30-SECOND TEXT

Jane Sidell

London has always thrived on trade, from local whaling in the seventeenth century to global commerce in the nineteenth century.

VILLAGES

the 30-second tour

Outside the medieval cities of London and Westminster lay monastic estates, manors, fields, woodland and villages, comprising a dependant and commercial network, serving the lord of the manor or monastery but also supplying the urban population with food and other necessities. Some villages held charters granting markets, for instance Barking's market dates from 1175. Many villages such as Dulwich, Stratford and Islington were engulfed long ago, while others were abandoned during the Black Death (1348–49), but some historic vestiges survive, like Highgate Village. Under the Tudors, great houses were built along the Thames joining London to Westminster, while peripheral villages such as Clerkenwell were swallowed after the Dissolution of the Monasteries in 1538–40. This act of Henry VIII led to extensive tracts of rural land being built upon over the next century, followed by the laying out of the West End under Charles II; grand estates were built and new districts such as Piccadilly and Covent Garden appeared, subsuming villages like Knightsbridge. In the Georgian era, aristocrats' desire for London estates led to architectural masterpieces such as Bedford Square. As growth flowed along the Thames and the roads into London, riverside settlements such as Wapping and Chelsea were absorbed into the urban mass.

3-SECOND SURVEY
Absorption of villages took centuries, from the period of medieval land enclosures, but the majority were absorbed following the Industrial Revolution and the complete change in London's economy.

3-MINUTE OVERVIEW
Railway construction in the mid-nineteenth century led to the almost wholesale absorption of rural villages surrounding central London by making it possible to commute from new suburbs such as 'Metroland', named after the Metropolitan Railway. Vast amounts of housing were built alongside railways, consuming land and turning rural pastures into fields of brick in areas such as Deptford, Camden and Kentish Town.

RELATED TOPICS
See also
THE GREAT ESTATES
page 46

TERRACES & SQUARES
page 48

THE SUBURBS
page 52

3-SECOND BIOGRAPHY
P. G. WODEHOUSE
1881–1975
Internationally acclaimed author who immortalized Dulwich Village under the pseudonym Valley Fields in many of his published works

30-SECOND TEXT
Jane Sidell

London is a polycentric city, its ancient villages creating a huge network of miniature centres.

REFUGE

the 30-second tour

3-SECOND SURVEY
As a potentially anonymous and certainly cosmopolitan urban setting, London has for centuries offered political, religious and other forms of refuge.

3-MINUTE OVERVIEW
London's population has overshadowed all other British cities and most European ones since the seventeenth century, a fact driven by the high rate of immigration to the city. Much of this has been international, from Loyalists during the American Revolution to Italians, Germans and French during the political crises of the 1830s and 40s. By 1910, 27,400 Germans, 11,300 French and 11,000 Italians were living in London, along with 140,000 Jews.

As a former centre of empire, nexus for maritime trade and offering potential seclusion or anonymity within its streets, London has always offered refuge for those fleeing from harm or seeking a place of greater political, religious or even sexual tolerance. Periodic influxes of large numbers of immigrants have left a particular imprint on the life of the city, from seventeenth-century Protestant Huguenots escaping persecution in France to the later émigrés of the French and Russian Revolutions. British liberties also offered safety for radicals fleeing political persecution, such as the Chinese nationalist Sun Yat-sen or Karl Marx, who famously found intellectual refuge in the British Museum's Reading Room. Before the Aliens Act (1905), thousands of Jews fleeing eastern European pogroms found a home in London, notably in Whitechapel, and several thousand more were able to find refuge from Nazi Germany in the 1930s. During World War II not just individuals, but entire governments in exile also set up in London, from the Czechoslovakian president in Putney to the Polish government in Portland Place. These influxes added to London's cultural life and helped to create today's cosmopolitan city. London has always offered other forms of refuge, notably the gay clubs and pubs of Soho or Vauxhall.

RELATED TOPIC
See also
MARITIME LONDON & EMPIRE
page 26

3-SECOND BIOGRAPHIES
KARL MARX
1818–83
German economist, journalist and revolutionary socialist, who sought refuge in London in 1849

SUN YAT-SEN
1866–1925
Chinese revolutionary, who in 1896 was detained in the Chinese legation in London before his release following a campaign in *The Times*. Yat-sen was subsequently the first president of the Republic

EDVARD BENES
1884–1948
President of the Czechoslovakian government in exile, 1939–45

30-SECOND TEXT
Matthew Shaw

People from all over the world have been attracted by the refuge this comparatively open and tolerant city has provided.

BUILDING LONDON

BUILDING LONDON
GLOSSARY

baroque Artistic style developed in Italy from the late sixteenth century that emphasized movement, flamboyance and exuberance.

the Blitz Early phase of World War II (September 1940 to May 1941) when the German Air Force, the Luftwaffe, embarked on the strategic bombing of British cities. The name derives from Blitzkrieg, German for 'lightning war'.

Changing of the Guard Military ceremony performed at the Queen's London residence, Buckingham Palace, approximately every other day, in which the Old Guard hands responsibility for protecting the palace to the New Guard.

Dissolution of the Monasteries, 1536–40 The seizure of all monastic lands and property by Henry VIII following the Reformation, when the Church of England split from the Roman Catholic Church.

Gothic Revival Artistic style originating in mid-eighteenth-century Britain before spreading across the globe, which drew inspiration from the Gothic art and architecture of 'native' medieval sources, often in deliberate contrast to Continental classicism.

green belt Area of protected rural (non-urban) land around major cities in Britain implemented under mid-twentieth-century planning laws to limit urban sprawl.

mews Small streets often situated behind larger thoroughfares originally designed to accommodate stables but which have since been converted into residential dwellings.

model cottage/dwellings New economical housing type promoted by charitable institutions in the nineteenth century to alleviate the acute problems facing the urban poor.

neoclassical Artistic revival of styles and iconography from classical antiquity that developed in the late eighteenth century and endured until the early twentieth century.

Queen Anne style Style of architecture popular during the reign of Queen Anne (1702–14) during the English baroque and characterized by ornate decorative features and a flamboyant use of red brick. The style enjoyed a revival at the end of the nineteenth and early twentieth centuries.

the Restoration The restoration of the English monarchy in 1660 under Charles II following the English Civil War, and often referring to his entire reign up to 1685.

the Royal Society Scientific academy established in 1660 to promote and advance the study of science in all its forms.

semi-detached A structure comprising two houses that share a party (dividing) wall.

stucco A finish made of cement, sand and lime mixed with water and applied to masonry to create a flat surface or decorative features and often painted white.

villa A detached or semi-detached residence in a rural or suburban setting possessing an air of pretension.

THE EAST & WEST ENDS

the 30-second tour

3-SECOND SURVEY
Underneath the surface both the East and West Ends share a history of migration, cosmopolitan culture and entertainment beyond the walls of the ancient City.

3-MINUTE OVERVIEW
What caused the different historical trajectory of East and West? Partly land ownership – the West End was developed on the lands of great aristocratic estates, the East on former Church estates (surrendered under Henry VIII's Dissolution of the Monasteries). Covent Garden served as the model for West End development by large estate holders from the mid-sixteenth century. The East End was always more fragmentary and dominated by development of the docklands.

There are two sides to London in the popular imagination. The West End of stuccoed squares and terraces, high fashion, world-famous restaurants, and stories from the bright lights of the theatre and opera. Then there's the East End of narrow lanes, pubs, street food from around the world, industrial dwellings, 'Jack the Ripper' and the underworld. Yet the histories of East and West run in parallel. They appeared as suburbs in the sixteenth century, the West End attracting those who wanted to be close to the Palaces of Westminster, the East End those needing the sea ports and docklands, escaping the direct authority of the Corporation of London. The West End was always more than wealth and entertainment, many of its residents engaging in manufacturing, trade and artistic production. Its different quarters – Bloomsbury, Soho, Fitzrovia and others – have fluctuated in fortune and perhaps only Belgravia and Mayfair retain their status as elite addresses. The East End has as long a history of salubrious residential quarters, and its theatres and music halls once competed with those of the West. But it has always been more cosmopolitan, and Spitalfields, Stepney, Poplar and West Ham, more than any other areas of London, were wracked by the Industrial Revolution and destruction in the Blitz air raids of World War II.

RELATED TOPICS
See also
TWO CITIES
page 24

REFUGE
page 30

TERRACES & SQUARES
page 48

IMPROVEMENTS
page 50

THEATRELAND
page 130

CRIME
page 142

30-SECOND TEXT
Nick Beech

Popular depictions of the East and West Ends contrast the commercial cosmopolitanism of the East with the pursuit of entertainment and leisure in the West.

ROYALTY

the 30-second tour

Today Britain's royal family

wields few actual powers, but performs various largely symbolic constitutional roles and acts as a powerful magnet for Britain and London in particular. Buckingham Palace is the family HQ. Its neoclassical facade, facing the Mall, dates from 1913. What lies behind was created mostly in the mid-nineteenth century, Queen Victoria having resolved to make the palace her London base. Prior to this, the royal court had various homes: Westminster Hall in the medieval period, followed by Whitehall Palace and St James's Palace. Buckingham Palace is a working building, hosting state occasions and attracting over half a million visitors annually. Of its 775 rooms, the Queen and her circle occupy only nine. Across the Mall stands Clarence House, the mini-mansion of Prince Charles, while the Princes William and Harry, and other family members, live in Kensington Palace. Surveys suggest that roughly one in five British people, including several leading London politicians, are republicans. However, those in the tourism business, together with those who flock to the Changing of the Guard ceremony, or who linger, misty eyed, at the Princess Diana Memorial Fountain, dismiss republicanism as pure folly. Once it was considered treason, a crime that inevitably led to another former royal stronghold, the Tower of London.

3-SECOND SURVEY
Buckingham Palace is the ceremonial hub of Britain's royal family, but is only one of a network of royal residences dotted around London.

3-MINUTE OVERVIEW
Inside the Banqueting House on Whitehall, designed by Inigo Jones in 1619, is an ornate ceiling painted by Peter Paul Rubens, celebrating the benign reign of James I. Outside is a bust of his son, Charles I. The painting was one of the last things Charles saw before he was beheaded by Parliamentarians in 1649, heralding the first and only republican phase in British history for over a thousand years. It lasted just 11 years.

RELATED TOPICS
See also
ROYAL ACADEMY
page 78

PROTEST
page 92

3-SECOND BIOGRAPHIES
QUEEN VICTORIA
1819–1901
British monarch whose reign coincided with a period of unprecedented growth in Britain and its Empire

QUEEN ELIZABETH II
1926–
Born in Bruton Street, Mayfair, she ascended to the throne in 1952, and in 2015 became the longest reigning monarch in British history

30-SECOND TEXT
Simon Inglis

The Royal family have occupied all manner of palaces in London over the last millennia and only comparatively recently been based in Buckingham Palace.

PARLIAMENT

the 30-second tour

Never mind the West End; some of the best theatre in London is to be found inside the Houses of Parliament (*parlement* being an Anglo-Norman word meaning conversation, or debate). In 1834 a fire destroyed the old sprawling medieval buildings – only Westminster Hall survived. A competition for a new parliament was won by Charles Barry and Augustus Pugin, whose grandiose Gothic pile, the Palace of Westminster, took 30 years to complete (1840–70). Today, this complex of buildings is a UNESCO World Heritage Site, although its future is uncertain. Much of the Victorian fabric is in acute need of restoration, a process that could take many years to complete, at a cost of billions of pounds. The legislative chamber, the House of Commons, is called the 'Lower House'. Its members (MPs) are elected by voters divided into 650 constituencies across the country, 73 of them in London. The adjoining House of Lords is called the 'Upper House', even though its powers are severely limited and, unlike any other major democracy, none of its members are elected. To enter either chamber, the public must first pass through the medieval magnificence of Westminster Hall, where England's parliament established itself in the thirteenth century. The ancient walls shout out 'Know your place!' Comes the echo: 'Power to the people!'

3-SECOND SURVEY
Britain's Houses of Parliament have operated from a site in Westminster, on the River Thames, for over 750 years.

3-MINUTE OVERVIEW
Many people refer to the clock tower at the Houses of Parliament as 'Big Ben'. In fact, Big Ben is the nickname given to the bell inside the tower. At almost 2.7 metres (9 feet) in diameter it is the largest bell ever cast by the Whitechapel Bell Foundry, whose current premises in east London, well worth visiting, date back to 1670. One reason for Big Ben's distinctive sound is that months after it was hung in place in 1859 a crack appeared.

RELATED TOPICS
See also
TWO CITIES
page 24

THE BATTLE OF THE STYLES
page 64

LONDON COUNTY COUNCIL
page 66

PROTEST
page 92

3-SECOND BIOGRAPHIES
SIR CHARLES BARRY
1795–1860
Architect, best remembered for the Gothic splendour of the Houses of Parliament

AUGUSTUS WELBY
NORTHMORE PUGIN
1812–52
Architect and designer who argued for a return to a medieval Gothic style and designed the interior of the Palace of Westminster

30-SECOND TEXT
Simon Inglis

Westminster has hosted parliamentary debate since the thirteenth century.

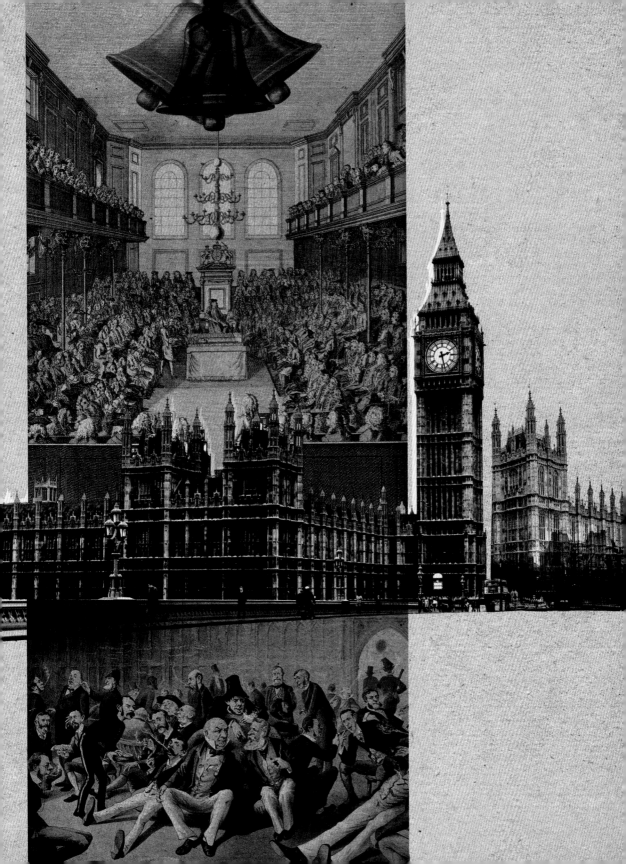

1633
Born in Fleet Street, London

c. 1644
Attends Huntingdon Grammar School (the former school of Oliver Cromwell)

1651
Enters Magdalene College, Cambridge

1655
Employed in Sir Edward Montagu's household as secretary

1660
Awarded post of clerk to the Navy Board

1665
Elected Fellow of the Royal Society

1684
Elected President of the Royal Society

1703
Dies in Clapham, London

SAMUEL PEPYS

Samuel Pepys was born to John Pepys, a tailor, and Margaret, daughter of a Whitechapel butcher, in London in 1633. Though his origins were modest, he would eventually inherit a minor estate in Huntingdonshire, where he spent some of his childhood and attended grammar school. Pepys was academically able and joined Magdalene College, Cambridge in 1651, completing a Bachelor's degree and eventually a Master's by 1655. When he returned to London, he was employed by Edward Montagu (later Earl of Sandwich) and proved himself a clerk of some talent, increasingly exerting influence in the Navy where he was more capable and adept than any of his rivals. His ability to marshal and give account of complex administration brought acclaim and he was awarded Fellowship and subsequently Presidency of the Royal Society. Throughout his later life Pepys formed a substantial library, kept entire to this day at Magdalene College. But Pepys's fame derives from a quite different activity.

From 1660, Pepys began writing a diary, which he sustained for nine years. He was, perhaps, fortunate to live in London as it passed through the most dramatic of political and material transformations – including the Great Plague of 1665, the Great Fire of 1666 and the subsequent reconstruction. But it is Pepys's unusual precision in describing these events, and the candour he displays in accounting of his own actions and those of others that makes him the greatest of London diarists, outweighing his friend John Evelyn (who otherwise conducted a much richer intellectual life).

As well as providing details of the inner workings of some of the most significant institutions and authorities in London (it was Pepys who delivered the news to Charles II of London's burning), Pepys's diary is filled with the daily delights and distractions of Restoration London – the theatres, music, fashions, arts, science, politics and religious life, but also daily routines. It also provides insight into the life of an ambitious, intelligent, sexually promiscuous Londoner who experienced all the city might offer, from the king's confidence to imprisonment in the Tower, music playing or surgery, dining on fine foods and victualling of the Navy, travelling rough seas and cobbled roads, and resting at night with another diary entry prepared.

Pepys abandoned his diary in 1669, fearful that impairment to his vision would result in blindness. Later unfinished works, brief memoirs and reports survive, but Pepys was unable to produce work of the quality and sustained brilliance of his diary. He died in 1703.

Nick Beech

FIRE!

the 30-second tour

Fire has dramatically altered

London's landscape, causing terrible destruction and stimulating architectural renewal. There were major early conflagrations, such as that begun on Pentecost in 1135, but even today, schoolchildren can immediately recite 1666 as the year that – in four terrible days – a great fire swept through the medieval City of London. Only six deaths were recorded, but the effect on buildings was catastrophic – over 13,000 houses, nearly 90 parish churches and St Paul's Cathedral were lost. All from a spark in a bakery on Pudding Lane. Christopher Wren had visions of a grand rebuilding but the need for speed meant that London kept much the same street plan, which is still legible today. Wren did, however, get his new, baroque-style St Paul's, and London's architecture would never be the same: jetties (projecting upper floors) were prohibited, sash windows had to be set back, and timber gave way to brick and stone. In 1834 the Palace of Westminster burned and was rebuilt in the new Gothic Revival style, influencing London's architecture throughout Queen Victoria's long reign. It also led to the founding of the London Fire Brigade in 1865. When the Blitz shook the city to its core in 1940–41, heroic architects kept watch on the roof of St Paul's, knowing that Londoners' morale relied on its survival.

3-SECOND SURVEY
Great fires in the capital, from 1666 to the Blitz, destroyed buildings and lives, but also encouraged a new architectural spirit as London rebuilt.

3-MINUTE OVERVIEW
During the Blitz, almost 20,000 people were killed in London and huge swathes of the city were destroyed. Bomb damage maps meticulously record the level of damage to buildings across the capital and explain pockets of post-war infill today. The losses led to wartime planning legislation and the birth of the listing system, which would identify and protect the most important buildings in post-war reconstruction. This would be shaped by bold city planning and a new modernist architectural spirit.

RELATED TOPICS
See also
MODERNISM
page 68

MAPPING LONDON
page 152

3-SECOND BIOGRAPHIES
SIR CHRISTOPHER WREN
1632–1723
Drew up a grand plan for rebuilding London after the Great Fire, but only his masterpiece cathedral was built

SAMUEL PEPYS
1633–1703
Graphically depicted the sights and sounds of the Great Fire in his diary

CHARLES HOLDEN
& WILLIAM HOLFORD
1875–1960 & 1907–75
Devised the City of London Plan (1946–7), which opened up and protected views of St Paul's

30-SECOND TEXT
Emily Gee

Conflagrations have shaped London over the centuries as much as humans have.

River Thames

THE GREAT ESTATES

the 30-second tour

The West End of London is dominated by 'estates' of streets and houses developed for profit by landowners who ranged from kings to aristocrats, charities, corporations and commoners. This pattern began in Bloomsbury Square; developed around 1661 by the Earl of Southampton, it formed the cornerstone of the Bedford Estate. By 1800, most of the map south of the 'New Road' (now Marylebone and Euston Roads), and east of Park Lane was filled in by interlocking landlords, with an acceleration after 1770. The painted stucco palaces of Regent's Park and the Grosvenor family's properties in Belgravia and lowlier Pimlico came later. Development brought slow but steady returns from 'ground rents'. The houses were subject to leases with whole streets 'falling in' at the same time, conventionally after 99 years, thus giving future generations the chance to rebuild en bloc. The smartest houses faced into garden squares with 'mews' for horses at the back, and there was always a range of house sizes. Land was set aside for churches to add respectability, while the Bedford Estate in Bloomsbury maintained its exclusivity by refusing to allow pubs or shops.

3-SECOND SURVEY
Historic London property was created by aristocratic landowners who gave their names to streets and squares.

3-MINUTE OVERVIEW
Some of the great estates are still held by the families who first developed them. Street names tend to derive from titles and residences, so that you know you are on Bedford land, for example, if you see the names Russell (the family name), Tavistock, Endsleigh and Woburn (country residences). However, the Dukes have now been joined by PLCs and Gulf wealth funds as modern estates have been built by commercial developers.

RELATED TOPICS
See also
THE EAST & WEST ENDS
page 36

TERRACES & SQUARES
page 48

THE CLASSICAL & BAROQUE
page 60

3-SECOND BIOGRAPHIES
JOHN GWYNN
1713–86
Architect who wrote *London and Westminster Improv'd* (1766) urging landowners to make better and more architecturally imposing developments

JOHN SUMMERSON
1903–92
Historian of architecture. His *Georgian London* (1945) unlocked the story of the great estates

30-SECOND TEXT
Alan Powers

As London grew, large swathes of the surrounding countryside were purchased by developers and these estates were converted into streets and squares.

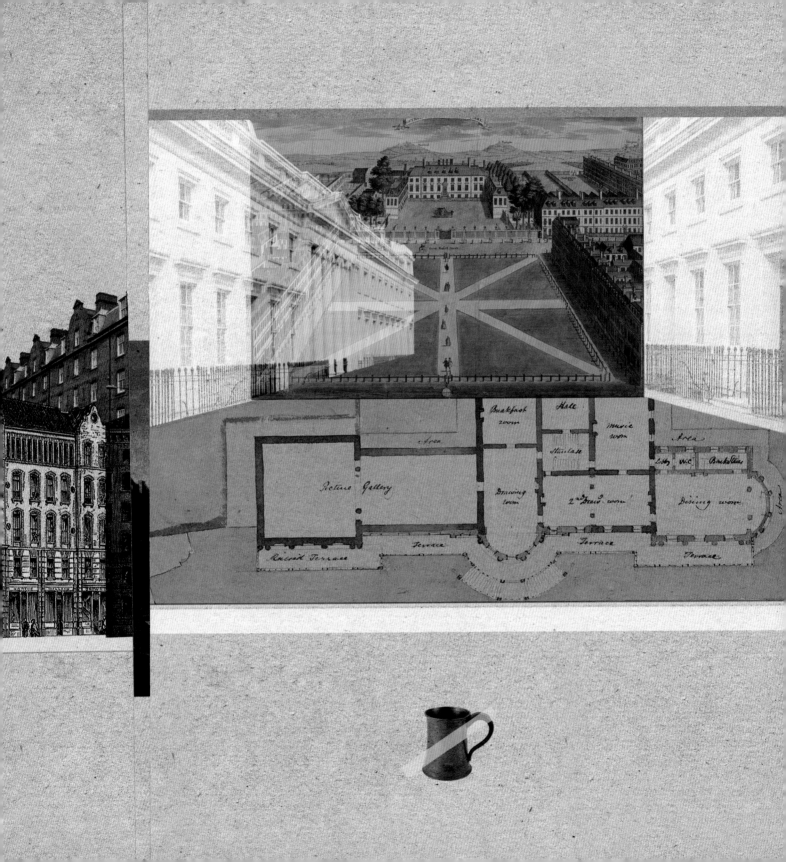

Picture Gallery

Raised Terrace

Area

Breakfast room

Drawing room

Terrace

Hall

Staircase

Music room

2nd Draw.g room

Terrace

Area

Library W.C. Back Stairs

Dining room

Terrace

Area

THE SUBURBS

the 30-second tour

The detached villa surrounded by private grounds in a leafy street provided space, privacy, health and cleanliness, as well as nature in gardens and smallholdings. The trend was pioneered in St John's Wood in the early 1800s and became an aspirational way of life. Cheap trains made longer commuting distances viable for the artisan worker, resulting in the 'Bye-Law Suburbs', or 'Workman's Villas' with long rows of solid two-storey basement-free terraces, complete with bay windows. These formed the next growth ring of London up to about 1910 – monotonous but now desirable residences. In Chiswick, Bedford Park (1870s) was an artistic precursor of the Edwardian architect-designed garden suburb. In reaction came the wider-frontaged semi-detached houses of vaguely vernacular character, forming a broader growth ring curtailed in 1938 by the Green Belt, and the target of undeserved abuse from architects and intellectuals. During this time, the London County Council was building 'out-county' estates of similar low density and monotony. Post 1945, the County Council favoured 'mixed development' of some tall blocks and some lower ones, while the private sector diversified into flats as well as houses, reaching an architectural and landscaping peak with the Span estates by Eric Lyons.

3-SECOND SURVEY
Suburbs aim to give the benefits of town and country in combination. London's loose planning structure encouraged their growth for all income levels.

3-MINUTE OVERVIEW
Suburbs and transport are interlinked. Tube lines control house prices, but environmentalists fret over the emissions of so many car journeys in daily life. The wide verges and long gardens may no longer relate to people's needs, but suburbs are better for biodiversity than agricultural land. They are also staging posts on the upward route of integration for immigrant populations.

RELATED TOPICS
See also
VILLAGES
page 28

LONDON COUNTY COUNCIL
page 66

RAILWAYS
page 108

3-SECOND BIOGRAPHIES
GEORGE & WEEDON GROSSMITH
1847–1912 & 1854–1919
Invented suburban comedy couple, Charles and Carrie Pooter, in *The Diary of Nobody* (1892)

JOHN BETJEMAN
1906–84
Poet Laureate and wry celebrator of suburbs, particularly in the documentary *Metroland* (1973)

ERIC LYONS
1912–80
Architect who invented Modernist suburban living with developers Span

30-SECOND TEXT
Alan Powers

Modernization liberated the new middle classes from the city centre.

3-SECOND
London's
social hous
considered
materials,
and carefu
help impro
conditions

3-MINUTE
Around 19
of the type
telephone
types of w
employed
who in turi
somewher
to live. In t
elite ladies
chambers,
residential
developed
lodging ho
working- a
women. Th
type featu
tiny bedro
sitting and
foster cam
a new com
working w

FIRST FLOOR PLAN

ARCHITECTURE

ARCHITECTURE
GLOSSARY

Archigram Avant-garde group of architects established in the 1960s whose futuristic projects and progressive ideas, typified by the Plug-In City (1964), provoked debates, combining architecture, technology and society.

Art Deco A decorative artistic style popular in the 1920s and 1930s defined by geometrical shapes, symmetrical design and highly stylized natural forms.

Arts and Crafts Progressive artistic movement established in Britain in the late nineteenth century that spread rapidly throughout the world, emphasizing the social and economic benefits of traditional crafts and trades over modern industrial production methods.

baroque Artistic style developed in Italy from the late sixteenth century that emphasized movement, flamboyance and exuberance.

buttress A mass of masonry built against a wall to counteract lateral forces from structures above, such as roofs.

classical From or making reference to the arts, culture and traditions of classical antiquity, notably Greece and Rome.

Cubism Artistic style developed in the early twentieth century that emphasized formal structure, combined different views of a subject and reduced form to pure geometric outlines or 'cubes'.

the Enlightenment Philosophical movement developed in the eighteenth century that emphasized reason and the critical reappraisal of existing ideas and political, religious and educational institutions.

Gothic Revival Artistic style originating in mid-eighteenth-century Britain before spreading across the globe. It drew inspiration from the Gothic art and architecture of 'native' medieval sources, often in deliberate contrast to Continental classicism.

listed buildings Buildings of historic or architectural interest afforded varying degrees of protection by being placed on a statutory list administered by relevant heritage bodies in England, Scotland and Wales.

Palladian A style of Renaissance architecture derived from the buildings and written works of Andrea Palladio (1508–80). Notable for symmetrical designs and use of classical harmony, its first practitioner in Britain was the seventeenth-century English architect Inigo Jones. Palladian principles and elements later became an essential part of the vocabulary of neoclassical architecture across Europe.

pendentive Method of construction that allows a circular dome to be built over a square room or an elliptical dome erected over a rectangular room.

Postmodernism Critical response in all forms of art from the 1970s to the doctrines, principles and practices of Modernism.

the Renaissance The fundamental revival of art, literature and learning in Europe beginning in the fourteenth century that defined the transition from the medieval period to the modern world.

the Stuarts Turbulent reign of monarchs from 1603 to 1714 during which the United Kingdom was formed.

THE ADVENT OF ARCHITECTURE

the 30-second tour

RELATED TOPICS
See also
THE CLASSICAL & BAROQUE
page 60

ROYAL ACADEMY
page 78

SCENES OF LONDON
page 80

3-SECOND SURVEY
Classical architecture was unknown in London until Inigo Jones at the beginning of the seventeenth century – it would become the dominant style for the next 200 years.

3-MINUTE OVERVIEW
Many buildings in London appeared with symmetry, classical proportions and decorative motifs derived from antiquity before Inigo Jones's famous designs in Whitehall and Greenwich. But Jones was the first to return from Italy with printed treatises that codified the rules of architecture, and with original drawings by Italian masters such as Andrea Palladio. Jones's library transformed London's architecture as much as his buildings, establishing architecture, for the first time in England, as an intellectual pursuit.

In 1614, James I appointed a costume and theatre designer as Surveyor to the King's Works. His name was Inigo Jones and he revolutionized English architecture. Having previously only designed large theatrical productions called 'masques', Jones had little experience of designing buildings. However, touring Italy, Jones learned of the architecture of antiquity and the Italian Renaissance, the technique of draughtsmanship, and rules of proportion, symmetry and the classical orders. Jones's designs for Banqueting House (1619–22), Queen Anne's House (1616–37) and St Paul's Church (1631–33), were admired throughout Europe. Jones developed a unique classical language, strict in proportions, rigorous in composition and delicate in decoration. He also established the role of the 'architect' as responsible for design; master not of a craft, such as stonemasonry or carpentry, but of drawing. Jones's fate was tied to the Stuart Court, and with the beheading of Charles I, his influence waned. His colleague John Webb inherited Jones's library and drawings but could not exert the same influence on King Charles II. Another 50 years would pass, until the arrival of Colen Campbell and Lord Burlington, for Jones and his Palladian architecture to achieve full dominance of design in London.

3-SECOND BIOGRAPHIES
INIGO JONES
1573–1652
Son of a Welsh cloth worker and originally designer of large theatrical works for the royal court. Inspired by his tours of Italy, Jones brought classical architectural design to Britain for the first time

JOHN WEBB
1611–72
Joined Jones's office in 1628. His relationship to Jones was always more than professional – referring to Jones as his 'uncle', Webb married into the Jones family

30-SECOND TEXT
Nick Beech

Inspired by classical Italian architects, Inigo Jones's work in London was admired throughout Europe.

THE CLASSICAL & BAROQUE

the 30-second tour

Eschewing strict rules of classical architecture, the architects of the English baroque were highly inventive. Christopher Wren, Nicholas Hawksmoor, John Vanbrugh and James Gibbs produced architecture of exceptional quality and singularity after the Great Fire of London. Wren designed St Paul's Cathedral and most of the City's churches, including the exquisite interior of St Stephen Walbrook. Hawksmoor used a great library of images from antiquity, from Persia to Rome, to compose his architecture. While some of the best baroque design of the period can be found in civil and military buildings (such as the Ordnance Board Building, attributed to Vanbrugh), the notable contribution to London's landscape is in church architecture. Classical motifs were married to medieval church plans to produce extraordinary works, none more so than Hawksmoor's designs for Christ Church Spitalfields, St George's Bloomsbury and St Anne's Limehouse. By the early nineteenth century, and with the emergence of John Nash and John Soane, a new inventiveness in London's architecture emerged: Nash with his picturesque landscaping of Regent's Park and grand sweep of Regent Street to Piccadilly and Haymarket, Soane with his extraordinary development of the pendentive dome, breaking once more from the hold of a strict classicism.

3-SECOND SURVEY
The baroque architecture of London appeared after the Great Fire of London and is remarkable for its invention and display of new ideas.

3-MINUTE OVERVIEW
As baroque architects attempted to develop new ideas for architectural design they drew on a wide range of traditions, incorporating medieval and non-classical architectures from antiquity (Egyptian, Persian and other pagan architectures). The baroque movement in architecture was informed by the Enlightenment principle, of the Royal Society, that knowledge derives not from written authority but from practical experience.

RELATED TOPICS
See also
FIRE!
page 44

THE ADVENT OF
ARCHITECTURE
page 58

CHRISTOPHER WREN
page 62

THE BATTLE OF THE STYLES
page 64

3-SECOND BIOGRAPHIES
NICHOLAS HAWKSMOOR
c. 1661–1736
Architect who worked with Wren and Vanbrugh. Was responsible for some of the greatest churches of his period

JOHN SOANE
1753–1837
Architect with a unique approach to design best displayed at his eponymous museum and at Dulwich Picture Gallery

30-SECOND TEXT
Nick Beech

Wren deployed advanced scientific study in the resolution of his design for St Paul's dome.

1632
Born in East Knoyle,
Wiltshire, on 20 October

1650
Studies Latin and
Aristotle at Wadham
College, Oxford

1657
Appointed Professor of
Astronomy at Gresham
College, London

1661
Elected Savilian Professor
of Astronomy at Oxford
University

1663
Founding member of the
Royal Society

1669
Appointed Surveyor
of the Royal Works,
a role he held until 1718

1673
Knighted for services to
the Crown

1680
Becomes President of the
Royal Society

1723
Dies on 25 February
and is buried in St Paul's
Cathedral, the Latin
inscription on his
gravestone reading:
'If you seek his memorial,
look about you.'

CHRISTOPHER WREN

Every age has its heroes, but few figures stand out as conspicuously, even in the tumultuous seventeenth century, as Christopher Wren – architect, politician and polymath. Wren will forever be regarded as one of Britain's most celebrated architects, primarily for his design of St Paul's Cathedral in the heart of the City of London, but his achievements go far beyond this singular structure that for so long dominated and defined London's skyline.

Wren lived a comfortable if sickly childhood as the only surviving son of Christopher Wren (senior) and Mary Cox. Educated at home, he had a natural gift for mathematics. In 1650 he began studying at Oxford University, where he received his MA in 1653 and continued his research until his appointment as Professor of Astronomy at Gresham College, London (1657–61). It was here, on 28 November 1660, that he gave the inaugural lecture for the 'learned society', which, after receiving royal approval in 1663, became the Royal Society. In 1661 he returned to Oxford as Savilian Professor of Astronomy.

Wren's scientific interests ranged widely from astronomy to medicine, but it was the nascent professional art of architecture that would concentrate his many talents. In the mid-1660s, he received his first architectural commissions for the Sheldonian Theatre, Oxford (1664), and a chapel (1665) for Pembroke College, Cambridge. A tour to France and Italy in 1665 ignited his passion for the baroque, which featured in his plans for the reconstruction of London's dilapidated Gothic St Paul's Cathedral. However, in 1666 the Great Fire of London tore through the city, destroying thousands of homes, shops and, crucially for Wren, most of its churches and St Paul's. If ever there was a person in the right place at the right time, it was Christopher Wren in September 1666. Within weeks he drafted a plan for London that proposed the complete reorganization of its street layout in a modern manner, with broad straight thoroughfares and grand piazzas. Although his plan was not adopted, his appointment as Surveyor of the Royal Works in 1669 secured his position as the most influential architect in the country for half a century.

The design and construction of St Paul's Cathedral, completed in 1711, would dominate a lifetime's work that also included the Monument to the Great Fire (1676), the Royal Observatory at Greenwich (1676), Cambridge University's Trinity College Library (1692), the Royal Hospital in Chelsea for retired soldiers (1692), Greenwich Naval Hospital (1696) and 51 London churches.

Edward Denison

THE BATTLE OF THE STYLES

the 30-second tour

In 1836 architect Augustus Pugin published a book, *Contrasts*. A recent convert to Roman Catholicism, Pugin had a simple message: classical architecture was mean, degenerate and pagan, and medieval architecture was splendid, superior and godly. The pointed arches, buttresses, decorated surfaces and irregular facades of medieval architecture signalled both a preferred style and a natural form for the Christian church. In mixing an aesthetic with a moral debate, Pugin ignited the 'battle of the styles', underlining a nationalist argument for the 'gothic' with his design for the Houses of Parliament (1834) with Charles Barry. Where a previous generation of architects had been happy to use one style or another, now hard lines were drawn – an architect had to choose. When John Ruskin published *Seven Lamps of Architecture* (1849) the argument was won: the 'Gothic Revival' had triumphed. William Butterfield's All Saints Margaret Street with its banded brick and extraordinary decorative interior became the model for ecclesiastical architecture. But it was London's new civic buildings, and philanthropic projects such as schools, tenements and libraries, that took neo-Gothic form most readily: G. E. Street's Royal Courts of Justice, Alfred Waterhouse's Natural History Museum and George Gilbert Scott's Midland Grand Hotel.

3-SECOND SURVEY
Amid fears of moral decay, London's architects turned away from classical design to a medieval, Gothic style.

3-MINUTE OVERVIEW
'The Battle of the Styles' was a phrase coined in reference to a protracted and by all accounts messy contest over the design of new government offices in Whitehall (Westminster) between 1856 and 1860. As this contest played between political factions, 'Gothic' represented conservativism, 'classical' liberalism. In truth, stylistic preference was always politically ambivalent and the moral writing of Pugin and Ruskin – though powerful – was less influential than those advocates had hoped.

RELATED TOPICS
See also
PARLIAMENT
page 40

IMPROVEMENTS
page 50

3-SECOND BIOGRAPHIES
AUGUSTUS WELBY NORTHMORE PUGIN
1812–52
Architect and designer who argued for a return to a medieval Gothic style of design

WILLIAM BUTTERFIELD
1814–1900
Architect whose highly controversial design for All Saints Margaret Street served as a model for neo-Gothic church design

JOHN RUSKIN
1819–1900
Art and social critic who championed craftspeople and opposed classicism

30-SECOND TEXT
Nick Beech

John Ruskin was a key player in the battle between classical and Gothic design.

LONDON COUNTY COUNCIL

the 30-second tour

3-SECOND SURVEY
From quaint through dull to sometimes scary, the LCC helped to shape London's architecture for nearly a century.

3-MINUTE OVERVIEW
In the early 1950s, LCC communist architects and sympathizers favoured a conservative Arts and Crafts-derived style, while the political moderates wanted extreme Brutalism. This strange reversal was symptomatic of indulgence in architectural politics rather than attending to accountability or user feedback that has left the LCC's reputation less than glowing. Ultimately, central government was responsible for regulating all kinds of buildings and their budgets. It could have been better, but we won't see its like again.

In 1889, the London County Council (LCC) replaced the Metropolitan Board of Works covering 28 boroughs excluding the City, with powers to fund infrastructure and service functions. From 1965 it became the Greater London Council, extending to outer boroughs, until it was abolished in 1986. In its earliest incarnation, the Council was dominated by members of the Progressive Party who prioritized replacing slums with better quality housing, such as the Boundary Street Estate, and built 'out-county' cottage estates, such as Totterdown Fields, as well as fire stations and schools. The Arts and Crafts design ethos of the in-house architects was influenced by W. R. Lethaby, the architect who was appointed Art Inspector at the LCC in 1894. Neo-Georgian style dominated the interwar decades, but after 1945 Modernism took over, as LCC Architects became the biggest architectural office in the world. The Royal Festival Hall and housing projects, such as Alton East and West in Roehampton, where rival teams favoured milder and stronger versions of Modernism in an Arcadian landscape, became widely known. Successive chief architects Robert Matthew, Leslie Martin and Hubert Bennett gave many young architects their early chances, but the brightest tended to leave for independent practice.

RELATED TOPICS
See also
THE SUBURBS
page 52

MODERNISM
page 68

BRUTALISM
page 70

3-SECOND BIOGRAPHIES
WILLIAM EDWARD RILEY
1852–1937
First Architect to the LCC, who established a tradition of teamwork by radical young design staff

J. LESLIE MARTIN
1908–2000
Probably the most influential man in post-war architecture, worked at the LCC from 1946–56

EDWARD HOLLAMBY
1921–99
Senior LCC Housing Architect 1949–62

30-SECOND TEXT
Alan Powers

The LCC was responsible for planning, housing, education, the fire brigade and tramways.

MODERNISM

the 30-second tour

England's Arts and Crafts

movement turned nostalgic after 1900 and the stylistic initiative for change passed to Continental Europe. A few 1890s pioneers, such as Charles Holden, designer of several Underground stations, morphed into Moderns, but it was mostly a style for the young, influenced by abstract art and an obsession with sunlight, split between following fashion and faith in social progress through design. 'Cubist' villas were condemned for looking like factories with flat roofs and white walls, while purists derided 'Moderne' (now called Art Deco), which made the style decorative. England caught up after 1930, with help from foreigners. In 1934, Berthold Lubetkin from Tblisi via Paris, put penguins on twirly ramps at London Zoo and designed Britain's first Modernist medical centre in Clerkenwell, in the former London Borough of Finsbury. Canadian architect Wells Coates put intellectuals in minimal flats at Lawn Road Flats. Refugees from Hitler included Walter Gropius and Erich Mendelsohn, who built houses side by side in Old Church Street, Chelsea, before leaving for the US. Peter Moro stayed on to design the interiors and facades of the Royal Festival Hall. After the war, Modernism became almost normal, but bred a new variant style called Brutalism.

RELATED TOPICS
See also
BRUTALISM
page 70

HIGH TECH
page 72

EXHIBITIONS
page 118

3-SECOND SURVEY
Cool to look at and chilly to live in, Modernism liberated structure and the psyche, but couldn't stop English rain from falling.

3-MINUTE OVERVIEW
Architectural styles change regularly, but Modernism was a step change equivalent to stone building replacing timber. It was driven by ideology as well as fashion, and intended to change the world. Compassionate soft Moderns contested with hard ones – would ruthless efficiency and economy or human values come out on top? Would a style without decoration continue to have long-term appeal after the initial stimulus of clearing away the past?

3-SECOND BIOGRAPHIES
WELLS COATES
1895–1956
A leader of the movement, whose work included Lawn Road (Isokon) flats and flats at 10 Palace Gate, Gloucester Road

BERTHOLD LUBETKIN
1902–89
Master of concrete and surface design, designer of Highpoint flats, London Zoo buildings and Finsbury Health Centre

PETER MORO
1911–98
Built schools, housing and his own Blackheath house in post-war London

30-SECOND TEXT
Alan Powers

The Modernist style housed both London's intellectuals and its zoo animals.

BRUTALISM

the 30-second tour

RELATED TOPICS
See also
LONDON COUNTY COUNCIL
page 66

MODERNISM
page 68

HIGH TECH
page 72

This emotive word of obscure origin (it has nothing to do with brutality) describes characteristics of Modern architecture after 1950: truth to materials (no stuck-on finishes); quirky shapes defying conventional form and avoiding prettiness or delicacy; and attention to people's movement pathways inside and outside the building. Brutalism is mainly identified with reinforced concrete, but also included brick, steel and timber. It can only be understood as a younger generation's reaction to the milder phase of Modernism that dominated from the mid-1930s to the Festival of Britain (1951) and seemed over-obsessed with a smart but potentially tacky look. Brutalism looked back to the original heroes of Modernism, such as Le Corbusier, whose more expressive post-war buildings gave the movement most of its visual signatures, especially the use of rough ('brut') concrete. It also reflected the social and artistic morality of Victorian Gothic and Arts and Crafts. Brutalism spread as a way of thinking and designing across the board, generating the next wave of styles including Archigram, High Tech and Postmodernism from its melting pot of ideas. Many architects now labelled Brutalist (such as Lasdun, Spence, Stirling and Gowan) rejected the label.

3-SECOND SURVEY
More tough love than cruelty, Brutalism was an existentialist cry for humanity in an increasingly robotic world.

3-MINUTE OVERVIEW
Reyner Banham asked 'ethic or aesthetic?' in his book, *The New Brutalism* (1966). Brutalism aspired to a new architectural morality, but one that mainly found expression in aesthetic terms and could thus be self-cancelling. Almost forgotten before 2000, the B word has snowballed back into public awareness to describe anything big or chunky. The term's negative connotations have hindered public understanding of buildings such as the Smithson-designed flats, Robin Hood Gardens.

3-SECOND BIOGRAPHIES
P. REYNER BANHAM
1922–88
Historian and critic who first named Brutalism in the press and wrote its intended epitaph in his 1966 book

ALISON & PETER SMITHSON
1928–93 & 1923–2003
Star Brutalists who designed the smooth Economist Group building in St James's Street

30-SECOND TEXT
Alan Powers

Alison and Peter Smithson were labelled Brutalist in 1952, and tried to own its meaning, but it swiftly spread throughout the architectural canon.

HIGH TECH

the 30-second tour

Britain's precocious engineering

tradition, visible in the railway infrastructure and grand exhibition halls of the Victorian period, was revived in the later twentieth century's High Tech architectural movement. High Tech buildings in London celebrate innovative materials, express their structure and are flexible in plan. The landmark Lloyd's building (Richard Rogers Partnership, 1982–88) helped to cast the image of the City in a new modern light, yet its soaring atrium acknowledged its Victorian neighbour, Leadenhall Market. Not just reserved for offices and industry, some of London's sleekest private houses are High Tech, such as the Hopkins House (1976) in a Hampstead conservation area, defined by flexible planning and materials borrowed from commercial traditions. Even the most mundane of activities, such as grocery shopping, can be done within a striking High Tech box in Camden Town. Here the Sainsbury's supermarket (Nicholas Grimshaw and Partners, 1988) holds its own with a parade of bold steel piers and residential pods alongside a G. F. Bodley church and the Regent's Canal. The tradition of blending old and new is also seen in Portcullis House, the offices for MPs designed by Michael Hopkins and Partners (1998–2001), where environmentally conscious design echoes the roofscape and perpendicular windows of the Houses of Parliament.

3-SECOND SURVEY
The High Tech movement celebrated Britain's great tradition of engineering and pioneered a new architecture that was functional, expressive and futuristic.

3-MINUTE OVERVIEW
Ironically, one of London's most famous High Tech buildings, the Lloyd's building (1988), is steeped in tradition. Built for London's oldest insurer, the 'inside-out building' dramatically expresses its services in shiny external steel toilet pods, lifts and ventilation shafts. Its interior was inherently flexible to accommodate changes in business practice. The soaring glazed atrium with dizzying escalators contrasts with the Georgian boardroom, imported from the previous Lloyd's building. It is one of the city's youngest Grade I listed buildings.

RELATED TOPICS
See also
MODERNISM
page 68

BRUTALISM
page 70

ENGINEERING
page 106

3-SECOND BIOGRAPHIES
LORD RICHARD ROGERS
1933–
Works include the Millennium Dome and Wimbledon glass and steel house for his parents

LORD NORMAN FOSTER
1935–
Works include 30 St Mary Axe ('The Gherkin')

SIR MICHAEL &
LADY PATRICIA HOPKINS
1935– & 1942–
Works include the addition to the former Financial Times building, Bracken House and London 2012 Velodrome

30-SECOND TEXT
Emily Gee

High Tech buildings are daringly futuristic but often nod to history and context.

ARTS & CULTURE

bohemian An artistic character whose lifestyle and attitude to work are free from conventional rules and practices.

Camden Town Group Group of artists based in London's northern suburb of Camden whose depictions of urban life in the early twentieth century came to define an important period of English art before World War I.

Chartists Working-class activists established in 1836 to campaign for political reform and the rights of the working classes.

debtors' prison Jails in which people who owed money to public or private firms were incarcerated until their debt could be paid.

Dickensian Resembling the period, style and often squalid conditions of nineteenth-century Britain, and in particular London, shown in the writings of Charles Dickens.

Downing Street Street off Whitehall in central London containing the residences of the Prime Minster (No. 10) and the Chancellor of the Exchequer (No. 11).

Gordon Riots, 1780 Anti-Catholic protest led by Lord George Gordon, President of the Protestant Association, fuelled by the Catholic Relief Act of 1778, which led to widespread rioting and looting across London.

Gothic Revival Artistic style originating in mid-eighteenth-century Britain before spreading across the globe. It drew inspiration from the Gothic art and architecture of 'native' medieval sources, often in deliberate contrast to Continental classicism.

Great Ormond Street Hospital Pioneering children's hospital established in central London in 1852 to provide dedicated inpatient care to children.

hackney carriage A form of taxi distinguished from other taxis by its special licence held by the driver that allows them to 'ply for hire' or stand in a rank.

Peasants' Revolt, 1381 Uprising among peasants of Kent and Essex that resulted in a march on London led by Wat Tyler and the unprecedented capture of the Tower of London. The young King Richard II negotiated with the peasants, though his concessions were later retracted and Tyler was killed by the Lord Mayor of London.

the Reformation Separation of the Church of England from the Catholic Church in the sixteenth century precipitated by many factors, including the effect of the Protestant Reformation in Europe and by Henry VIII's desire to divorce his first wife, Catherine of Aragon, which the Catholic Church forbade.

the Renaissance The fundamental revival of art, literature and learning in Europe beginning in the fourteenth century that defined the transition from the medieval period to the modern world.

rookeries Impoverished and crowded tenement houses that proliferated in the nineteenth century due to rapid industrialization and intense urbanization.

suffragette movement Women's organization established in the late nineteenth century that became a political movement in the early twentieth century campaigning for women's rights and in particular the right to vote.

workhouse Institutions established in the fourteenth century and abolished in the twentieth century that provided accommodation for the impoverished and destitute in return for unskilled manual labour.

ART PATRONAGE

the 30-second tour

3-SECOND SURVEY
For centuries, London's art scene has thrived on – as much as been shaped by – the patronage of the city's wealthiest and most influential residents.

3-MINUTE OVERVIEW
The Royal Academy (RA), founded in 1768 by 34 eminent artists and architects, sought not only to exhibit the nation's best work but also to promote art through education and public debate. A century after its foundation, the RA moved to Burlington House, Piccadilly, where it still remains one of the nation's leading art institutions. The RA possesses Britain's oldest fine art library and hosts public debates and the annual Summer Exhibition.

Over three centuries, London went from being a centre for the arts in Britain to a global capital. The origins of this prodigious rise can be traced to the sixteenth century, when the Reformation and the European Renaissance loosened the tight grip that the Church and the monarchy had on art. The growth of London's aristocracy and their capacious residences paralleled the commoditization of art and the use of their homes as private galleries. Art was also used as a force for social and moral good. The eighteenth-century painter and satirist William Hogarth was a founding Governor of London's Foundling Hospital and encouraged its use as a venue for art exhibitions and recitals, including regular performances of Handel's *Messiah*. The patronage of art through exhibitions in the manner of (and an alternative to) the Paris salons was a feature of eighteenth-century London. The Dilettante Society (1732), the Foundling Hospital, the Society of Artists of Great Britain (1761) and the Royal Society for the encouragement of Arts, Manufactures and Commerce (RSA, 1754) presaged the eventual establishment of the Royal Academy in 1768. The founding of the Arts Club (1863) and the rival Chelsea Arts Club (1891) continued the patronage of the arts throughout the nineteenth century.

RELATED TOPICS
See also
SCENES OF LONDON
page 80

MUSEUMS & GALLERIES
page 102

3-SECOND BIOGRAPHIES
JOSHUA REYNOLDS
1723–92
A founder member and the first President of the Royal Academy of Arts in 1768

JOHN SOANE
1753–1837
Architect and Royal Academy professor who converted his house in Lincoln's Inn Fields into a museum for his huge collection of art, architectural artefacts and antiquities

CHARLES SAATCHI
1943–
One of Britain's leading art patrons, he famously sponsored the Young British Artists throughout the 1990s

30-SECOND TEXT
Edward Denison

The Royal Academy, whose first President was Joshua Reynolds, has occupied Burlington House since 1867.

SCENES OF LONDON

the 30-second tour

London has been depicted by
visual artists since the sixteenth century.
Each has brought their own perspective and
presented very different faces of the city.
Canaletto's depictions of the Thames present
London as if it were a version of his native
Venice. The French printmaker Gustave Doré,
working 150 years later, captured late-Victorian
industrial London as a dark satanic city. But
London has produced its own artists too.
William Hogarth's work was often of a moral
theme, depicting social scenes that still resonate
today: *A Rake's Progress*, *Industry and Idleness*,
Beer Street and *Gin Lane* provide rich depictions
of London life and landscape. George Cruikshank,
James Gillray and Thomas Rowlandson – all born
in London – presented the eighteenth-century
city as a roaring, boisterous world of people
mixing, fighting and filling streets, lanes, public
houses and coffee shops. The vicious bite of
these caricaturists was replaced in the late
nineteenth and early twentieth centuries with
social insights concerned with simple reflections
on the landscapes of London life; the Camden
Town Group, for example, depicted the interiors
of everyday homes, cafés and shops. Perhaps
the most famous London artist is J. M. W. Turner,
whose paintings present the fog and smoke,
railways and shipping of the working city as a
majestic play of light.

3-SECOND SURVEY
London has been
presented as a sublime,
pretty, wonderful and
wicked city by a succession
of artists since the
sixteenth century.

3-MINUTE OVERVIEW
Depictions of London
often tell us as much
about the artist as they
do about London itself.
But regardless of whether
an artist has communicated
the atmosphere, the social
life, the politics, the
architecture, the events,
or simply the colour and
form of the city, so often
London is portrayed as
a centre of excess and
restlessness.

RELATED TOPICS
See also
ART PATRONAGE
page 78

MUSEUMS & GALLERIES
page 102

3-SECOND BIOGRAPHIES
GIOVANNI ANTONIO CANAL
'CANALETTO'
1697–1768
Venetian artist whose works
were particularly popular
among British 'Grand Tourists'

WILLIAM HOGARTH
1697–1764
Influential painter, printmaker
and art critic, produced a series
of prints depicting London life

J. M. W. TURNER
1775–1851
Painter whose Romantic
landscapes, particularly in
oil, contributed to the
transformation of European
landscape art

30-SECOND TEXT
Nick Beech

*From Canaletto to
Hogarth, artists
have long been
inspired by London.*

1812
Born in Landport, Hampshire

1824
Dickens's father enters Marshalsea debtors' prison, Southwark

1827
Begins work as a clerk in Gray's Inn

1832
Begins to publish as the parliamentary sketchwriter, Boz

1836
Serialization of *The Pickwick Papers* and begins work on *Oliver Twist*

1843
Publishes *A Christmas Carol*

1852
Begins philanthropic support for Great Ormond Street Hospital

1856
Purchases Gad's Hill Place in Higham, Kent

1870
Dies in Higham, Kent

CHARLES DICKENS

It is difficult to imagine a city as closely associated with an author as London is with Charles Dickens. Smog, pickpocket-infested rookeries, the lower reaches of the Thames and taverns serving roast beef and ale are all summoned in the tourist image of a London that is, well . . . *Dickensian*. Much of this is gone, or never quite existed, but, as numerous commemorative plaques attest, the city is still full of sites closely associated with the author. As a child, Dickens spent several years in Southwark debtors' prison, forced to work in a blacking warehouse near Charing Cross and then Covent Garden; an experience that helped to form his social consciousness. After clerking in Gray's Inn, his skills as a mimic took him to the edges of theatreland and the beginnings of his literary career as the parliamentary sketchwriter, 'Boz'.

Great novelistic success came with the serial publication of *Oliver Twist* and *The Pickwick Papers*, and was reinforced with a series of hugely successful works, which often drew on his intimate understanding of working-class London. Dickens's social and political views became increasingly apparent in his novels and in philanthropic projects, including constructing cottages in Shepherd's Bush for 'fallen women' and support for Great Ormond Street Hospital. In his novels he revealed the human costs of Victorian institutions, such as the workhouse, indicting society's attitudes towards poverty and the exploitation of workers.

As well as his moral vision, Dickens's power and popularity as a novelist lay in his linguistic exuberance and in his brilliant creation of a vast cast of characters which brought to life all of Victorian society. Chief among these characters is that of London itself, notably portrayed in the rookeries of *Oliver Twist* (1837–39), the London of government and debtors' prisons of *Little Dorrit* (1855–57) and the legal world of *Great Expectations* (1860–61). His writings also influenced the shape of London itself, with his depiction of the inhumanity of Fleet Prison in *The Pickwick Papers* partly leading to its closure in the early 1840s.

At his death he was mourned as the greatest novelist of his age. He requested that no statue of him be made, but his novels remain in print and are still critically and popularly regarded. Dickens's image of London also lives on in the dozens of films and numerous television dramas based on his works.

Matthew Shaw

FILM

the 30-second tour

For film-makers, London is a magnificent movie set bristling with ready-made props and scenes, from Gothic gables, classical colonnades and high-tech towers to cobbled streets, concrete jungles and verdant parks and gardens. London's most enduring cinematic depiction is its crime-ridden foggy Victorian streetscape immortalized in the film adaptations of Charles Dickens's novels and Arthur Conan Doyle's Sherlock Holmes stories. The Harry Potter series drew on the city's traditional characteristics when featuring George Gilbert Scott's Gothic-Revival masterpiece The Midland Grand Hotel, with Horace Jones's Leadenhall Market recast as Diagon Alley and the entrance to the Leaky Cauldron. Modern London has been the setting for some of the most memorable scenes in cinema history, from the dystopian casting of Charles Holden's Senate House as the Ministry of Truth in *Nineteen Eighty-Four* (1984) and Thamesmead in *A Clockwork Orange* (1971) to the comedic horror of *An American Werewolf in London* (1981) or capturing modernity's mood in The Beatles' *A Hard Day's Night* (1964) and the cult classic *Blow-Up* (1966). London's romantic side has also endured in film, from *My Fair Lady* and *Mary Poppins* (both 1964) to *Notting Hill* (1999), *Shakespeare in Love* (1999) and *Love Actually* (2003).

RELATED TOPICS
See also
SCENES OF LONDON
page 80

CHARLES DICKENS
page 82

THEATRELAND
page 130

SHERLOCK HOLMES
page 144

3-SECOND BIOGRAPHIES
ALFRED HITCHCOCK
1899–1980
One of the greatest film directors of the twentieth century, renowned for his masterful use of suspense

MICHAEL CAINE
1933–
One of Britain's most celebrated actors, born in Bermondsey, south London, and renowned for his strong London accent

30-SECOND TEXT
Edward Denison

London's depiction in film has made the city familiar to audiences worldwide.

LONDON

CAMERA
DATE   SCENE   TAKE

THE BLOOMSBURY GROUP

the 30-second tour

The Bloomsbury Group, a network of writers, artists, activists and dilettanti, began in Cambridge but crystallized in 1904 in Bloomsbury, then an unfashionable area of Georgian terraces and squares between Euston Road and Holborn. The men and women of the Bloomsbury Group were united by a revolt against social conventions and a belief in the power of ideas to change and improve the lives of others by rational thought, gender equality and breaking taboos. Their specialisms ranged from economics (John Maynard Keynes) through psychoanalysis (Adrian Stephen) to the better-known writing (Virginia Woolf, Lytton Strachey) and art (Roger Fry, Vanessa Bell, Duncan Grant). They were arguably Britain's chief creative and critical avant-garde before 1914. Private life and friendship were paramount, expressed in conversation and letters. Although they also spent time at their houses in the countryside, Bloomsbury remained an important geographical focus: it was cheap, bohemian and well situated for research and publishing. Fry's Omega Workshops, set up in 1913 in Fitzroy Square, set new French-inspired styles for interiors. Virginia Woolf's novels, especially *Mrs Dalloway* (1925), express the slightly delirious feeling of London life at the time – parties, domestic graces, and the interiority of private and public sadness after World War I.

3-SECOND SURVEY
Connected by family and friendship, the Bloomsbury Group was widely influential in many fields of culture.

3-MINUTE OVERVIEW
The Bloomsbury Group has suffered bad press from D. H. Lawrence onwards, accused of snobbery and mutual back-scratching. The 1970s and 1980s saw it return from obscurity and captivate scholars and public alike who wished they'd been there. It deserves a more balanced assessment, as the total range of thought and output is astonishing, even if highly uneven. Several of the houses lived in by the group survive in Gordon Square.

RELATED TOPIC
See also
TERRACES & SQUARES
page 48

3-SECOND BIOGRAPHIES
ROGER FRY
1866–1934
Introduced modern French art to London in 1910 and 1912, a thoughtful popularizer of all forms of art

VIRGINIA WOOLF
1882–1941
Learned, catty, endlessly fascinated by people, but also self-doubting to the point of death

JOHN MAYNARD KEYNES
1883–1946
Pioneer of demand-led thinking in economics, favouring public works subsidy to stimulate employment during depression

30-SECOND TEXT
Alan Powers

The Bloomsbury Group was made up of a constellation of artists including Virginia Woolf, Duncan Grant, Vanessa Bell and Roger Fry.

MRS DALLOWAY IN BOND STREET

MRS DALLOWAY said she would buy the gloves herself.

Big Ben was striking as she stepped out into the street. It was eleven o'clock and the unused hour was fresh as if issued to children on a beach. But there was something solemn in the deliberate swing of the repeated something stirring in the murmur of wheels and the shu

No doubt they were no on errands of happiness. There is much more to be sai s than that we walk the streets of Westminster. Big Ben to thing but steel rods consumed by rust were it not for the c 's Office of Works. Only for Mrs Dalloway the m ; for Mrs Dalloway June was fresh. A happy s not to his daughters only that Justin Par llow (weak of course on the Bench); flowe ng; the caw of rooks falling from ever so gh the October air— there is nothing to t ood. A leaf of mint brings it back; or a cu

Poor little wretch forward. Oh, right under the horses' nos d there she was left on the kerb stretchin mmy Dawes grinned on the further side.

A charming woman white-haired for her pink cheeks, so Scope as he hurried to his office. She stiffened rtmill's van to pass. Big Ben struck the t n stroke. The leaden circles dissolved in th t, inheriting, handing on, acquainted with ffering. How people suffered, how they su king of Mrs Foxcroft

OMEGA WORKSHOPS LTD·
33 FITZROY SQUARE W.I.
PORTLAND RD & WARREN ST STATIONS

MODERN PAINTINGS
(V.BELL·R.FRY·D.GRANT·M.GERTLER
N.HAMNETT·E.WOLFE)

DRESSES
(MLLE GABRIELLE)

NEW OMEGA POTTERY
(BREAKFAST & DINNER SERVICES)

EXHIBITION OPENS
OCT. 26

RED BUS, BLACK CAB

the 30-second tour

Red buses and black taxi cabs are the classic London combination, and for good reason. Most cities buy their buses and taxis off the shelf. But with London's twisting roads, stop-start traffic and heavy payload, only bespoke designs stand the strain. Bus passenger numbers have doubled since the 1980s and in 2014 London's buses drove almost half a billion kilometres (300 million miles). The rules for London buses were laid down in 1909. Vehicles had to be hard-wearing, simply engineered, with all parts being completely interchangeable. London Transport had its own engineers, research department and production lines, which in the 1950s created the world-famous Routemaster bus, with its iconic open rear platform. The Routemaster recently underwent a redesign, with the new model boasting three doors, two internal staircases and dashing diagonal front and rear windows. Similar attention has been paid to the design of black cabs (officially 'hackney carriages'). London's fleet of 23,000 cabs retain their curvy, roomy character, but will in future be powered by eco-friendly engines. One thing technology can never replace is 'the Knowledge'. This is the test – requiring knowledge of 320 routes, 25,000 streets and 20,000 landmarks – that all black cab drivers must take before getting their badge.

RELATED TOPICS
See also
RAILWAYS
page 108

THE UNDERGROUND
page 110

MAPPING LONDON
page 152

3-SECOND SURVEY
Such is the complexity and congestion of London streets that since 1909 buses and taxis have had to be specially designed to cope with the workload.

3-MINUTE OVERVIEW
'Hold very tight please!' Once the clarion call of London's 'clippies' (bus conductors) who swung daringly from the rail on the open platform of a Routemaster, this cry can now only be heard on Route 15 from Tower Hill to Trafalgar Square. Only ten of these classic buses still work London's streets, but of the 2,876 built between 1954 and 1968, incredibly over 1,200 survive elsewhere, owned by collectors, museums and bus companies as far afield as China and Australia.

3-SECOND BIOGRAPHY
THOMAS HEATHERWICK
1970–
London-born designer who wowed the world with his Olympic Cauldron during the opening ceremony for the 2012 Games. His distinctive remodelling of the classic Routemaster also debuted in London in 2012

30-SECOND TEXT
Simon Inglis

London prides itself on its efficient transport system and its design heritage, which come together in the world famous old and new Routemaster bus and the black cab.

PUNK

the 30-second tour

Punk was not born in London,

but the city swiftly became its spiritual home. The embryonic energy of early punk emanating across the Atlantic found the perfect host amid the economic misery and social boredom of mid-1970s London. Punk was a cultural attitude fervently embraced by disillusioned and disenfranchised youth, finding its most potent expression in music – raw, angry and primordial. The soundtrack to British punk rock was forged in London's dingy pubs and seedy nightclubs – El Paradise, 100 Club, the Marquee and the Roxy – before reverberating around the globe. Punk's most influential band was the Sex Pistols, comprising four teenagers from across London brought together by the impresario Malcolm McLaren who owned a fashion boutique called Sex on Chelsea's King's Road with his partner, fashion designer Vivienne Westwood. Today, decades after punk exploded in all its swearing, sneering and spitting fury into British popular culture, the theatrical image of the angry figure clad in Dr Marten boots, with brightly coloured hair and safety-pinned attire has become a symbol of London's counter-culture. Behind this stereotype, punk remains one of the most potent expressions in a long and quintessentially British tradition of opposing the establishment.

3-SECOND SURVEY
Punk may have been born in New York, but it made its home in London where it enjoyed an uproarious adolescence.

3-MINUTE OVERVIEW
Punk's dystopian vision of London was a consistent catalyst and compelling backdrop for some of its greatest anthems and the inspiration for many songs including: The Clash's 'London's Burning', 'White Riot', 'White Man in Hammersmith Palais' and 'Guns of Brixton'; 'Down in the Tube Station at Midnight' and 'A Bomb in Wardour Street' by The Jam; 'Dark Streets of London', 'Rainy Night in Soho' and 'London You're a Lady' by The Pogues; and Madness's 'We are London'.

RELATED TOPICS
See also
PROTEST
page 92

CLUBS
page 126

3-SECOND BIOGRAPHIES
JOE STRUMMER
1952–2002
Lead singer of The Clash and writer of some of the most critically acclaimed punk songs

JOHNNY ROTTEN
1956–
Lead singer of the Sex Pistols famed for his piercing sardonic gaze and green teeth that inspired his nickname

SID VICIOUS
1957–79
Sex Pistols' bassist and media antihero who died of a heroin overdose having been accused of murdering his girlfriend Nancy Spungen

30-SECOND TEXT
Edward Denison

Vivienne Westwood's boutique, Sex, was at the centre of punk's nihilistic style.

PROTEST

the 30-second tour

As the centre of political power

in Britain, London has always been a site of both peaceful and violent protest. Its dense network of streets has provided a theatre for marches, while public squares and greens have become spaces for gatherings and communal action, from the mass Chartist meeting on Kennington Common (1848) to the Poll Tax (1990) and the recent anti-austerity riots of Trafalgar and Parliament Squares. London also has a record of quieter vigils, whether outside Parliament or in front of national embassies, as well as the democratic tradition of the symbolic presentation of petitions to Downing Street. Such protests might have their roots in the Peasants' Revolt (1381) or the days of anti-Catholic violence known as the Gordon Riots (1780), but also draw on a lexicon of public gatherings, ranging from religious processions, public hangings and the knockabout hustings of the British electoral tradition. Although often male-dominated, the first quarter of the twentieth century was also peppered by the actions of the suffragettes, who burned down the refreshment pavilion at Kew Gardens and whose threat to public artworks caused radical changes to museum and gallery admissions. Today, London's spaces increasingly outlaw public protest, from Westminster Square itself to private developments such as Canary Wharf and King's Cross.

INNOVATION & LEARNING

INNOVATION & LEARNING
GLOSSARY

cabinet of curiosities Large collection of uncategorized artefacts housed in rooms or purpose-made buildings that were the antecedent to modern museums.

chronometer A timepiece engineered to achieve extreme precision and used at sea to determine longitude.

City of London A city and county of Britain governed by the City of London Corporation and covering a geographic area broadly defined by the walls of the Roman settlement, also referred to as the Square Mile.

comprehensive education System of state education introduced in Britain after World War II based on non-selective intake of pupils.

the Enlightenment Philosophical movement developed in the eighteenth century that emphasized reason and the critical reappraisal of existing ideas and political, religious and educational institutions.

Greenwich Observatory Royal Observatory based in Greenwich, east London, founded in the seventeenth century, which established the Prime Meridian that created Greenwich Mean Time.

Kew Gardens World's largest collection of living plants housed in the extensive grounds of the former Kew Park, southwest London, established in the eighteenth century by Lord Tewkesbury and later expanded by Augusta, Dowager Princess of Wales, to the exotic designs of Sir William Chambers.

livery companies Trade and craft associations based in the City of London also known as guilds, whose name derives from the uniforms that distinguished one livery company from another.

Modernist Adherent of modern ideas and theories, particularly those of the modern movement that, motivated by a rejection of tradition, dominated all forms of artistic expression in the twentieth century.

the Royal Society Scientific academy established in 1660 to promote and advance the study of science in all its forms.

Thames Estuary Area to the east of London where the Thames dispenses into the North Sea, characterized by extensive mudflats and marshland.

utilitarianism Moral movement established in the late eighteenth century and supported by leading theorists including Jeremy Bentham and John Stuart Mill that proposes a morally good deed is one that benefits the greatest number of people. Utilitarianism has had a major impact on political, economic and social theory ever since.

Wellcome Trust An independent global charitable foundation that funds scientific research dedicated to improving health.

EDUCATION

the 30-second tour

In England, the state has never been keen on taking responsibility for education, preferring instead to subcontract it to religious, charitable and commercial institutions. London's merchants, artisans, aristocrats, clergy and philanthropists filled the vacuum laudably. Since medieval times, the City of London's guilds and livery companies have primed young Londoners for a merchant life in the same way that St Paul's Cathedral and Westminster Abbey pioneered the city's religious education. St Paul's Cathedral School (1123) and Westminster School (1371) are London's oldest surviving schools. Charity joined the ranks of educational providers from the fifteenth century, with the establishment of the City of London School (1442), St Paul's School (1509) and Christ's Hospital (1552), which later incorporated the Royal Mathematical School (1673). Nineteenth-century industrialization and urbanization heralded a modern system of public education in London. Following the Public Elementary Education Act (1870) the newly established School Board for London erected fine school buildings all over the capital, many of which still survive, albeit converted into luxury apartments or offices. In the early 1930s London County Council pioneered 'comprehensive' education, which later became the national standard.

3-SECOND SURVEY
Forever a melting pot of people and ideas, London has a long educational tradition that has pioneered pedagogic developments in Britain and across the globe.

3-MINUTE OVERVIEW
University College London (UCL) was Britain's first secular university, established in 1826 as an egalitarian alternative to the elitist religious institutions of Oxford and Cambridge. Open to students of any race, creed or political persuasion, UCL was founded on the utilitarian principles of 'the greatest happiness of the greatest number' and was inspired and supported by the social reformer, Jeremy Bentham, whose clothed skeleton sits in a glass cabinet in the university's South Cloister.

RELATED TOPICS
See also
LONDON COUNTY COUNCIL
page 66

JEREMY BENTHAM
page 100

GLOBAL KNOWLEDGE
page 104

3-SECOND BIOGRAPHIES
SAMUEL WILDERSPIN
1791–1866
Pioneer of infant education and author of *On the Importance of Educating the Infant Poor* (1823)

SIR CHARLES REED
1819–81
MP for Hackney and Chairman of the London School Board, which pioneered a citywide system of education for London's poor

30-SECOND TEXT
Edward Denison

Christ's Hospital pupils today still wear the Tudor uniform of yellow stockings, bluecoat and breeches. London now has over 3,100 schools for 1.3 million pupils.

1748
Born in Houndsditch,
London

1760
Attends The Queen's
College, Oxford, at the
age of 12

1776
Anonymously publishes
*A Fragment on
Government*, a criticism
of the British government

1786
Travels to Russia and
conceives the idea of
the Panopticon with
his brother Samuel

1791
Publishes first work on
the Panopticon

1823
Co-founds political
journal the *Westminster
Review*

1832
Dies in Westminster,
London; his body is
preserved as an Auto-
Icon

1850
Bentham's preserved
skeleton is acquired
by University College
London where it remains
on public display

JEREMY BENTHAM

There are few areas of modern

life untouched by the thoughts and writings of Jeremy Bentham, the philosopher, jurist and founder of the school of thought known as utilitarianism. Born in Houndsditch, east London, in 1748, Bentham was a child prodigy who grew up to benefit from a private income, which after an early career as a lawyer allowed him to devote his life to a rational critique of the world and the institutions that he found around him. There were few areas of Georgian life that escaped his gaze. Most famously, Bentham's dictum 'the greatest happiness of the greatest number' became a shorthand encapsulation of his utilitarian philosophy. This critical test led him to make the case for democracy, prison reform, welfare, animal rights and the decriminalization of homosexuality. A deeply held concern for a rational response to social problems led him, amongst other innovations, to help create the Thames River Police, which greatly influenced Robert Peel's police reforms 30 years later.

Inspired by a visit to Prince Potemkin's Russia, Bentham began work on his great project of the Panopticon, which attempted to physically organize prisons under the gaze of a supervisor, allowing them to be cheaper and more humane. He received a grant for this scheme from the government, and planned a National Penitentiary at Millbank according to these principles, although the final building owed little to the Panopticon principle. Attracting an influential circle of admirers, Bentham's wider range of thought was disseminated around the world, and, after his death in 1832, developed by a group of important writers and theorists such as John Stuart Mill.

Bentham left instructions for his body to be given to medical science and then preserved as an 'Auto-Icon' for future generations. The padded-out and dressed skeleton, with the addition of a wax head, is now to be seen in University College London where it has resided since 1850, along with the majority of his writings, which amount to some 30 million words. Although Bentham is often closely associated with the University, and indeed appears in a mural by Henry Tonks in the main Flaxman Library giving approval to the architect's plans, he played no direct part in the campaign for the creation of the college, with the exception of purchasing one of the 1,000 shares in the new university.

Matthew Shaw

MUSEUMS & GALLERIES

the 30-second tour

London's penchant for museums and galleries – totalling just over 200 – has its roots in the eighteenth-century cabinet of curiosities. This form of display allowed aristocrats to showcase their latest acquisitions and let everyone know how well travelled, clever and wealthy they were. Pre-eminent was Sir Hans Sloane, an Irish physician who, on his death in 1739, bequeathed to the nation his vast collection, worth an estimated £80–100,000, for just £20,000. Sloane's gift became the basis of the British Museum, opened in 1759, and his books formed the nucleus of the British Library. His other specimens eventually helped create the Natural History Museum in 1860. This latter institution occupies imposing Victorian buildings alongside the Science Museum and Victoria & Albert Museum. Private donors helped establish the National Gallery on Trafalgar Square, among them the landscape artist and Chelsea resident J. M. W. Turner, who bequeathed over 1,000 pieces of his work. There are few areas of British life that have not been celebrated in a museum or gallery, with museums for all kinds of sports, toys, gardens, canals and even sewing machines, and galleries for paintings, cartoons and photography. Oddly, the most obvious topic – London itself – was not encapsulated in a museum until 1976, with the opening of the Museum of London.

RELATED TOPICS
See also
ART PATRONAGE
page 78

EXHIBITIONS
page 118

3-SECOND SURVEY
London has over 200 museums and galleries, covering an amazing range of subjects, periods and tastes, from great works of art to sewing machines.

3-MINUTE OVERVIEW
Many museums attract visitors not just for their collections, but also for their architecture. The Tate Modern is housed in a remodelled awe-inspiring mid-twentieth-century power station. The Great Court at the British Museum is covered by a stunning glazed canopy. And the Serpentine Sackler Gallery occupies a gunpowder store (built in 1805), with a curvaceous extension added in 2013. In each case, the juxtapositions of old and new constitute exhibitions in themselves.

3-SECOND BIOGRAPHIES
SIR JOHN SOANE
1753–1837
Architect and inveterate collector whose numerous artefacts gleaned from around the world are displayed in his beautifully preserved house in Lincoln's Inn Fields

MADAME MARIE TUSSAUD
1761–1850
French sculptor who set up her eponymous waxwork museum on Baker Street in 1835

SIR HENRY TATE
1819–99
Made his fortune from sugar and spent much of it on art, now seen in the gallery on Millbank that bears his name

30-SECOND TEXT
Simon Inglis

London's museums and galleries are second to none for their variety of subjects and artefacts.

GLOBAL KNOWLEDGE

the 30-second tour

Today the home for major museums, universities and institutions such as the Wellcome Trust and the Royal Society, London has for centuries been at the heart of global networks of knowledge. Its proximity to royal and government power encouraged the development of institutions such as the Greenwich Observatory and the Royal Society, while its coffee-house culture of debate helped to shape the development of the scientific method and of scholarly societies. In such a city, ideas could be tested and disseminated, while international trade brought a steady flow of written communication from savants around the world. London's commercial and imperial role also underscored the practical nature of intellectual exploration, from the commercial exploitation of foreign flora to the development of naval technology, such as the longitude-revealing chronometer. A series of great collectors, such as Sir Robert Cotton and Sir Hans Sloane, formed the foundation for several of London's foremost knowledge institutions, including Kew Gardens, the British Museum, the Natural History Museum and the British Library. This blend of commercial and scholarly endeavours can still be seen in London's physical presence in the internet age. It is no accident that the web giant Google chose King's Cross to be its new European home.

3-SECOND BIOGRAPHY
SIR HANS SLOANE
1660–1753
Collector and, from 1727, royal physician. The bequest of his collections to the nation formed the basis of the British Museum and, later, the Natural History Museum

30-SECOND TEXT
Matthew Shaw

London is home to many learned societies that have helped transform our understanding of the world, from life on earth to the depths of space.

3-SECOND SURVEY
Trade, developments in military technology and simple curiosity have placed London at the heart of the world's knowledge networks since at least the seventeenth century.

3-MINUTE OVERVIEW
The Royal Society can safely claim to be one of the world's oldest and most eminent scientific associations. It began with a gathering of polymaths at a lecture given by Christopher Wren in 1660 and gained royal approval in 1663 as 'The Royal Society of London for Improving Natural Knowledge'. Its published *Philosophical Transactions* established the idea of the peer-reviewed scientific journal, underpinned by the motto, 'Nullius in verba': take nobody's word for it.

ENGINEERING

the 30-second tour

The existence of modern London

is in large part a result of extraordinary feats of engineering, for as much as the Thames has always been the lifeblood of London, it has proved a challenge to domesticate. London Bridge was first erected in the thirteenth century, but it wasn't until Charles Labelye's Westminster Bridge, completed in 1750, that the river began to be engineered. That was soon followed by Kew (1759), Blackfriars (1769), Battersea (1773) and Richmond (1777). The Regent's Canal soon crossed London, connecting the docks of the East End to the Grand Union Canal and the provinces. Joseph Bazalgette's Victoria Embankment combined embankment of the river with a new underground railway and connection to a great sewage system – one that London relies on to this day. Further taming of the river occurred in the twentieth century with the construction of the Thames Barrier (1982) protecting London from flooding. In the twenty-first century Crossrail – an underground railway connecting outer west and east London and one of the largest and most complex engineering projects in Europe – presents a double engineering feat. The tunnelling has produced a mass of clay used to construct an island in the Thames Estuary, creating an artificial wild habitat for birds and a floodplain to protect London.

3-SECOND SURVEY
Modern London is the product of engineering, bridges, canals, docks, tunnels (for rail and sewage), barriers and even artificial islands.

3-MINUTE OVERVIEW
London's infrastructure is the product of great engineering feats. Along with the bridges and tunnels of London, one can observe mighty railway sheds, the tensile dome of the O2 Arena in Greenwich, the London Eye on the South Bank and the BT Tower – all made possible by civil, structural and mechanical engineers, whose institutes London is home to.

RELATED TOPICS
See also
THE THAMES
page 22

RAILWAYS
page 108

THE UNDERGROUND
page 110

3-SECOND BIOGRAPHIES
CHARLES LABELYE
1705–62
Engineered London's first modern bridge

WILLIAM HENRY BARLOW
1812–1902
Designed St Pancras station's train shed, then the world's largest single-span structure

JOSEPH BAZALGETTE
1819–91
Transformed London with a network of sewers and the Victoria Embankment

30-SECOND TEXT
Nick Beech

Today's sophisticated city could not function without its sewers, tunnels, bridges and barriers.

RAILWAYS

the 30-second tour

In 1836 London Bridge terminus
was opened to the public and so was created a
new kind of building and a new kind of Londoner.
Mid-nineteenth-century London was hit by a
succession of 'Railway Manias', as investors
flocked to sink capital into the new schemes
passed in Parliament by joint stock companies.
London Bridge was joined by Euston (1837) and
five more, including Paddington (1838–54),
Waterloo (1848) and King's Cross (1852). All
these were far outside the Cities of London and
Westminster, as the Corporation of London
and major estate holders refused to provide
freeholds to the railway companies. A second
wave beginning with Victoria (1862) and
concluding with Liverpool Street (1874) brought
the termini closer to the centre. The railways
allowed Londoners to move out to the suburbs,
creating the commuter. They also inaugurated
the great London hotels as for the first time
visitors arrived all at once in very large numbers.
Every terminus was also an advert for the railway
company – none more spectacular than the
Midland Grand Hotel of St Pancras Station,
outdoing its neighbour the Great Northern
Hotel of King's Cross. The peculiar pattern of
above-ground railway lines in London, with far
more south of the river than north, are a product
of the difficulties presented by tunnelling in
chalk and of belligerent landowners.

3-SECOND SURVEY
The introduction of
the railway to London
contributed to the city's
great geographic and
demographic expansion
in the nineteenth century.

3-MINUTE OVERVIEW
For many millions,
the stations of London
have served as the
first gateways to the
metropolis. All Londoners,
and many visitors and
guests, have experienced
at least some time spent
waiting for delayed trains
in one of the many termini.
In these moments, one
can admire the great
engineering feats of the
railway sheds, or the
many station characters
(Paddington Bear, Harry
Potter, Sherlock Holmes)
to whom Londoners have
become attached.

RELATED TOPICS
See also
IMPROVEMENTS
page 50

THE SUBURBS
page 52

ENGINEERING
page 106

3-SECOND BIOGRAPHIES
GEORGE THOMAS
LANDMANN
1779–1854
Military and civil engineer
and promoter of London and
Greenwich Railway

ISAMBARD KINGDOM BRUNEL
1806–59
Engineer who linked London
to New York under steam
power with his Great Western
Railway from Paddington to
Bristol and SS *Great Western*
from Bristol to New York

30-SECOND TEXT
Nick Beech

Since the age of steam,
railways have linked
London to the industrial
Midlands and North,
and now to Europe.

THE UNDERGROUND

the 30-second tour

One of London's most successful and endearing brands is the Underground's distinctive red roundel with a blue diameter line, first used in 1908. The world-famous underground railway was also the world's first: the Metropolitan Railway opened in 1863 as a cut-and-cover route from Paddington to Farringdon Street, an engineering feat that required many houses to be demolished and residents displaced. To avoid scepticism about travelling under the ground, stations like Baker Street were designed with natural lightwells to the platforms and gas lamps on the trains. Today, well over a billion passengers a year travel on the Tube, a nickname that came from the first of the deep-level 'tube' tunnels through London's susceptible clay in 1880. A complex series of other companies' lines in subsequent decades merged as the Underground Group in 1902. A masterwork of visual brand identity, beyond the roundel and Johnston sans-serif typeface, the architecture of the stations is just as distinctive: Leslie Green's 46 Edwardian ox-blood tiled facades, each in a different palette of interior tiles; Charles Holden's brick Modernist stations on the Piccadilly Line; and turn-of-the-millennium Jubilee Line stations, like the Piranesian concrete at Westminster.

3-SECOND SURVEY
London's underground railway was the world's first, opened in 1863, and thanks to a strong visual identify from the start, it is also the best known.

3-MINUTE OVERVIEW
The Underground has a fine reputation for commissioning art, particularly under Frank Pick in the early twentieth century. Evocative posters urged Londoners to go 'To The Zoo' and other uplifting locations newly reached by Tube. Finishes within stations include Harry Stabler's creamy tiles embossed with iconic London buildings at Aldgate East, and Eduardo Paolozzi's jazzy mosaics from the 1980s at Tottenham Court Road that introduce bold colour in the spirit of Harry Beck's iconic map.

RELATED TOPICS
See also
RAILWAYS
page 108

SUBTERRANEAN LONDON
page 140

MAPPING LONDON
page 152

3-SECOND BIOGRAPHIES
CHARLES HOLDEN
1875–1960
Designed a series of striking Modernist stations on the Piccadilly Line in addition to the London Underground headquarters at 55 Broadway

FRANK PICK
1878–1941
Commissioned the famous typeface and roundel

HARRY BECK
1902–74
Designed the groundbreaking Underground map in 1931

30-SECOND TEXT
Emily Gee

London's Underground has remained a pioneer of design, architecture and engineering.

BUSINESS & PLEASURE

BUSINESS & PLEASURE
GLOSSARY

basilica Building used for public administration in ancient Rome that became the prototype for early Christian churches with the incorporation of a nave, side aisles, transept and apse.

bay window A window protruding from the façade of a building, creating an alcove internally with oblique views of the street.

City of London A city and county of Britain governed by the City of London Corporation covering a geographic area broadly defined by the walls of the Roman settlement, also referred to as the Square Mile.

Modernism Artistic movement that flourished in the mid-twentieth century motivated by a rejection of tradition and the pursuit of modern ideas and theories.

Norman Conquest The conquest of Britain in 1066 by Duke William II of Normandy, later known as William the Conqueror, who defeated King Harold at the Battle of Hastings.

the Restoration The restoration of the English monarchy in 1660 under Charles II following the English Civil War, and often referring to his entire reign up to 1685.

Restoration comedy Form of comedy renowned for its lewd style and plot lines that flourished after the prohibition of theatrical performances during the Commonwealth era and remained popular throughout the Restoration.

Royal Mint The 1,100-year-old institution licensed to design and manufacture Britain's coins.

Savile Row Street in the district of Mayfair, central London, made famous by its high-quality bespoke tailors and clothiers.

South Bank An area of central London on the southern bank of the River Thames once occupied by the temporary Festival of Britain (1951), which now comprises the entertainment and commercial district that extends from Westminster Bridge to the National Theatre.

Square Mile The area of London broadly defined by the old Roman settlement and its wall and today administered by the City of London Corporation.

university boat race Annual boat race held on the River Thames since 1856 between the universities of Oxford and Cambridge.

PARKS, GARDENS & OPEN SPACES

the 30-second tour

When you are in the thick of the city it seems hard to believe that London ranks as the world's third greenest city, behind Singapore and Sydney. Yet when idling on the slopes of Hampstead Heath or even in some of the more secluded pastures of Hyde Park, it is equally hard to believe you are in a city at all. An amazing 38.4 per cent of London is public green space. This is made up of 122 heaths, commons and greens (Richmond Park being the largest); 600 municipal public parks (Finsbury Circus being the oldest, dating from the seventeenth century); 1,500 playing fields and 125 recreation grounds (including Hackney Marshes, which has 77 football pitches, the largest concentration in the world), plus dozens of garden squares, cemeteries and churchyards. And that does not include private gardens and no fewer than 108 golf courses. Londoners have been fighting to preserve open spaces since villagers outside the city walls started to hedge in the fields between Moorgate and Islington in the sixteenth century. The Victorians fought off developers with a series of Acts of Parliament and protection orders. Remember these doughty campaigners when you next lie down on the grass with the sounds of the city humming beyond the trees.

3-SECOND SURVEY
Amid all the buildings and bustle, over a third of London's land mass is taken up by green space that remains accessible to the public.

3-MINUTE OVERVIEW
Several of London's parks originated as playgrounds for kings, queens and their aristocratic friends. Hyde Park was originally a hunting ground for Henry VIII. In the early nineteenth century Regent's Park was designed as a private park for the wealthy residents of villas and terraces built around its perimeter. Finally local authorities started to lay out parks for the people, starting with Victoria Park, Hackney, in 1845, and Battersea Park in 1858.

RELATED TOPICS
See also
THE GREAT ESTATES
page 46

TERRACES & SQUARES
page 48

IMPROVEMENTS
page 50

ARENAS
page 124

3-SECOND BIOGRAPHIES
JOHN RUSKIN
1819–1900
London writer and critic, who said 'the measure of a city's greatness is to be found in the quality of its public spaces, parks and squares'

GEORGE LANSBURY
1859–1940
Socialist MP who tore down fences and opened up London's parks for the benefit of working men and women

30-SECOND TEXT
Simon Inglis

London boasts many magnificent public parks, such as Hyde Park and Regent's Park.

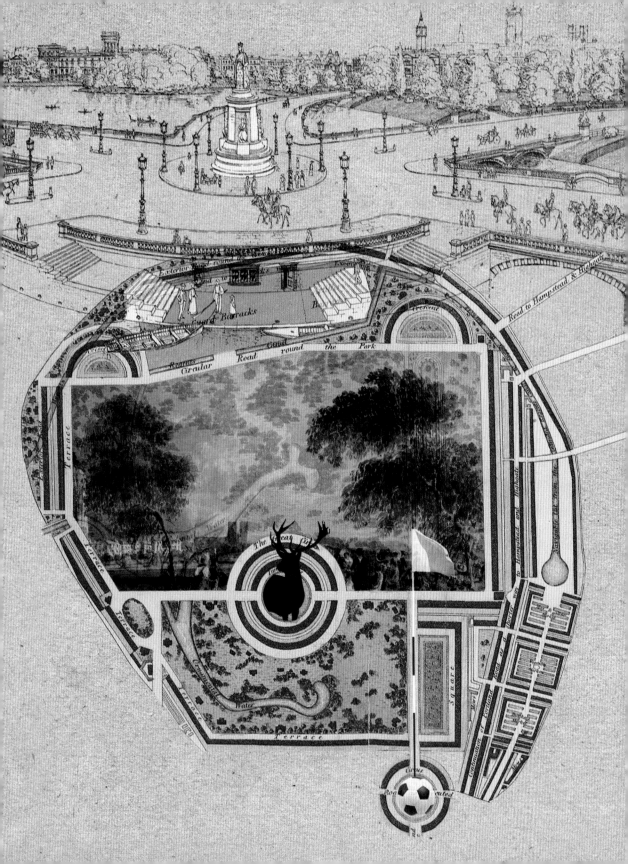

EXHIBITIONS

the 30-second tour

The Great Exhibition of the Arts

and Industries of all Nations of 1851, housed in Joseph Paxton's Crystal Palace, was a money-spinner that London's exhibition organizers have tried to emulate ever since. Its artistically more interesting successor of 1862, however, was a commercial flop. In 1908 the Franco-British Exhibition launched the White City, used for further shows before 1914, and best remembered for its funfair. In 1924–25, the British Empire Exhibition, a government-sponsored show with a trade mission masked by much patriotic and colonialist flummery, opened at Wembley in new classical-style concrete buildings, including the hilltop Stadium. The South Bank was the core of the 1951 Festival of Britain, with modestly Modernist pavilions, fountains and landscaping, a successful 'Tonic to the Nation' proclaiming liberal values and a new vision of nationhood at ease with modernity. The last big show to date was the Millennium Experience of 2000 on Greenwich Peninsula, imbued with a rather bossy and charmless populism typical of Tony Blair's New Labour party. Other major exhibition centres include Olympia and ExCel, providing homes for the many trade shows that London attracts.

Over the years several exhibitions have left a permanent mark on London's architecture.

MARKETS

the 30-second tour

London's markets are its citadels of commerce. For two millennia, markets have been the key nodes in a network of trade that grew to span the globe. The city's first market – the Forum – was part of the Roman basilica, one of the largest structures in Europe, sprawling over 2 hectares (5 acres) on the site of present-day Leadenhall Market. Its remains can still be seen in the basement of a local barber's shop. The origins of London's existing markets can be traced to the twelfth century, when the city regained its title as Britain's most important trading hub after the Norman Conquest. Trade fairs were established in the new settlement of Westminster and outside the old Roman walls at Smithfield, where meat has been continuously traded for over 800 years. In the thirteenth century coal, iron, wine, corn, salt and fish were sold in Billingsgate Market, which by the sixteenth century traded exclusively in fish and continues to do so today, though it was removed from the City in 1982. London's expansion in the seventeenth century presaged new fruit and vegetable markets in the East End at Spitalfields and in the emerging West End at Covent Garden, which lowered the tone of London's first Italianate piazza. Today, New Covent Garden Market, in Vauxhall, is the largest fruit, vegetable and flower market in Britain.

RELATED TOPICS
See also
ROMAN LONDON
page 18

MARITIME LONDON & EMPIRE
page 26

MONEY, MONEY, MONEY
page 122

SHOPPING
page 128

30-SECOND TEXT
Edward Denison

3-SECOND SURVEY
Markets are synonymous with many of London's most cherished landmarks and tourist destinations: Bermondsey, Borough, Camden, Haymarket, Spitalfields, Smithfield and Covent Garden.

3-MINUTE OVERVIEW
The City of London has long been a stronghold of trade, its street names echoing its early markets: Wood Street, Milk Street, Bread Street, Poultry Lane and Cheapside ('ceap' is Saxon for market). Livery companies – drapers, haberdashers, jewellers, mercers, skinners, saddlers – fiercely protected their trades. In 1327 the City's market rights were protected by Royal Charter, prohibiting any market within 6.6 miles of the City – the furthest distance someone could walk to and from market in a day to sell their wares.

London's markets have always thrived on the tension between high-society's pretensions and the public's subsistence.

MONEY, MONEY, MONEY

the 30-second tour

3-SECOND SURVEY
If it is true that money makes the world go round, then London must be the centre of the world.

3-MINUTE OVERVIEW
The language of money is embedded in London's colourful culture. Terms such as 'wonga' (coal) arrived with the Romany gypsies, but London's native fiscal tongue comes from Cockney rhyming slang. 'Dough' (money) derives from 'bread', the abridged version of 'bread and honey' (money). A pound was once called a 'saucepan' through the rhyming of 'saucepan lid' and 'quid' (an informal seventeenth-century term for pound), or 'nicker', which presented the obvious if cheeky pun for two pounds: 'pair of knickers'.

Since Roman times, the City has been London's beating heart and money its lifeblood, nourishing its financial and commercial institutions and imbuing every fibre in the fabric of its society. Manufacturing of money in London began in the seventh century, and between 1279 and 1810 the Royal Mint was housed in the Tower of London, but today money's impact is far more noticeable in its intangible rather than its tangible form. Until Canary Wharf was developed from the 1980s, London's financial district was confined to the Square Mile, an area broadly defined by the old Roman Wall. Standing proudly in the centre of the City at the convergence of six major roads is the Bank of England, the nation's principal financial institution. Founded in 1694, the Bank of England moved to its present location on Threadneedle Street in 1734 opposite the city's centre of commerce, the Royal Exchange, and Mansion House, the Lord Mayor of London's home. Later expansion led to the 'Old Lady of Threadneedle Street' occupying a 1.2-hectare (3-acre) plot and the building of plush additions designed by Sir John Soane, whose extraordinary impenetrable curtain wall still skirts the Bank's ground floor. The keys to the Bank's vault are nearly a metre (1 yard) long.

RELATED TOPICS
See also
ROMAN LONDON
page 18

TWO CITIES
page 24

MARKETS
page 120

3-SECOND BIOGRAPHY
ISAAC NEWTON
1643–1727
Appointed Warden of the Royal Mint in 1696 and Master in 1699, a position he held until his death

30-SECOND TEXT
Edward Denison

With over £3 trillion a day flowing through its banks, exchanges, insurance companies and other financial institutions, London is the world's leading financial centre.

ARENAS

the 30-second tour

Londoners love a spectacle.

In the twelfth century William Fitzstephen described ball games and horse races on the Smooth Field (now Smithfield). In the sixteenth century thousands attended jousting matches in Whitehall. By the eighteenth century the big draw was cricket at the Artillery Garden (still in use, on City Road). London's first attempt at an Olympic revival was in 1866. The gymnastics were staged in the German Gymnasium (still extant, by St Pancras Station). Next to the old BBC Media Village in White City you can see the location of the finishing line of the 1908 Olympic Marathon. Wembley Stadium hosted another Olympics in 1948. Rebuilt since then with a giant arch, Wembley is London's largest arena, holding 90,000. Most cities manage with one major multi-functional stadium. Not London. In addition to Wembley there is Twickenham (capacity 82,000), the home of rugby union; the 2012 Olympic Stadium at Stratford (60,000); and the Emirates Stadium (60,000), home of Arsenal – one of 14 professional football clubs in the city (more than any other apart from Buenos Aires). Similarly, not content with a single arena for Test cricket (like every other city), London has two: Lord's and the Oval. Wimbledon, meanwhile, hosts the world's only remaining Grand Slam tennis tournament still played on grass.

RELATED TOPICS
See also
EXHIBITIONS
page 118

PARKS, GARDENS & OPEN SPACES
page 116

ARENAS
page 124

3-SECOND SURVEY
London possesses more international sporting arenas in a wider range of sports than any other world city, including for football, rugby, cricket, athletics and tennis.

3-MINUTE OVERVIEW
There are around 780,000 seats spread amongst London's numerous sporting arenas, 22 of which hold more than 10,000 spectators. This compares with 146,000 seats in cinemas and theatres. Yet the most popular single event is the annual university boat race, held since 1829 between crews from Oxford and Cambridge. This draws crowds of up to a quarter of a million, standing, often precariously, along the banks of the River Thames or perched on bridges.

3-SECOND BIOGRAPHIES
THOMAS LORD
1755–1832
Wine merchant and professional cricketer who established Lord's Cricket Ground in Marylebone

ARCHIBALD LEITCH
1865–1939
Engineer who designed many British football grounds, for clubs including Chelsea, Arsenal and Tottenham. His best preserved grandstand, built in 1905, is at Fulham's Craven Cottage on the banks of the Thames

30-SECOND TEXT
Simon Inglis

London's sporting heritage has spawned world-famous names including Wimbledon and Wembley.

CLUBS

the 30-second tour

England is exceptional for its membership organizations serving a multitude of benevolent, cranky or self-advancing purposes. London's traditional clubs cluster in the West End, with the more socially exclusive in St James's Street or Carlton House Terrace, and the more architecturally magnificent in Pall Mall. Many still reflect their historic roots in politics or professions. They offer a 'home from home', with food and drink, libraries and other facilities. High Society clubs include Annabel's (1963), beneath the Clermont Club (gentlemanly gambling) in Berkeley Square. Visual arts clubs include the Langham and London Sketch Clubs (1838), the Art Workers' Guild (1884) in Bloomsbury and the Chelsea Arts Club (1890). Musical performances have flourished in club format. The Royal Philharmonic Society (1813) commissioned Beethoven's Ninth Symphony in 1827. Nightclubs, usually with dance bands, circumvented licensing laws. The Gargoyle Club in Dean Street, Soho (1925), displayed a major Matisse painting and, in 1979, it gave birth to the Comedy Store. Ronnie Scott founded his eponymous jazz club in Soho in 1959, while Heaven, a gay club underneath Charing Cross Station, was founded in 1979. The Ministry of Sound, opened in 1991 at Elephant and Castle, was London's first club dedicated to house music.

RELATED TOPICS
See also
THE EAST & WEST ENDS
page 36

ART PATRONAGE
page 78

3-SECOND SURVEY
Hidden in plain sight, some in magnificent palaces, some behind unmarked street doors – clubs serve as London's complex power structure and sources of pleasure, both innocent and guilty.

3-MINUTE OVERVIEW
Club membership usually depends on recommendation by two existing members, and a voting process either by committee or by the membership body. Historically, this was done with black and white balls placed in a polling box, hence 'black-balled' applicants deemed unsuitable. Women are still excluded from membership of several, mainly older, clubs, but women-only clubs have existed since the 1890s and have grown in number, with an emphasis on exercise facilities and cultural programmes.

3-SECOND BIOGRAPHIES
SIR CHARLES BARRY
1795–1860
Architect of two outstanding club houses in Italian Renaissance palazzo style, the Travellers (1832) and the Reform (1841)

MARK BIRLEY
1930–2007
Founder of Annabel's (named after his wife) and Mark's Club

30-SECOND TEXT
Alan Powers

London's clubs cater for every conceivable taste, from the classical finery of Barry's Reform Club to the neon revelry of Soho's jazz and strip joints.

SHOPPING

the 30-second tour

If England is a nation of

shopkeepers, then London is a suitably fitting capital, with Oxford and Regent Streets as its triumphal avenues. Long the home of markets and a port city with a constant flow of goods for sale, London's shopkeepers aided the consumer revolution of the eighteenth century, helping to set the fashion for clothing, porcelain or jewellery. The premier shopping street of the day, the Strand, introduced the first bay windows, allowing the shopkeepers' wares to be put on general display. By the early twentieth century, influenced by American modes of shopping, Harrods and Selfridges department stores had established themselves as destinations, and, with the introduction of public conveniences and cafés, they offered public spaces accessible to women, as well as job opportunities. Today, like most other cities, London is marked by the dominance of large chains, yet it still retains its own mix of luxury shops and shopping areas that still have their traditional character, such as the bespoke tailors of Savile Row. London's size and geography means that London has escaped the dominance of the shopping mall, despite several developments around the city such as Brent Cross in the 1960s, Bluewater in the 1990s, and the more recent and vast Westfield shopping centres in Shepherd's Bush and Stratford.

3-SECOND SURVEY
London has always been the place to spend money, and today its famous shopping streets exert a tremendous pull on millions of credit cards.

3-MINUTE OVERVIEW
Shopping as a leisure activity was largely created in the nineteenth century, notably in the impressive department stores. While many of the earliest ones were utilitarian, and existed as much to serve clients through catalogues, a series of innovations, such as lifts and escalators, marketing savvy and ever-changing window displays created institutions that were destinations in themselves.

RELATED TOPICS
See also
THE EAST & WEST ENDS
page 36

MARKETS
page 120

MONEY, MONEY, MONEY
page 122

3-SECOND BIOGRAPHY
HARRY SELFRIDGE
1858–1947
American retailer who opened Selfridges department store in Oxford Street in 1909

30-SECOND TEXT
Matthew Shaw

Shoppers love London and few stores epitomise this amorous relationship more than Harrods and Selfridges.

THEATRELAND

the 30-second tour

Theatres are thickly peppered across the zone east of Regent Street, south of Soho and west of Kingsway known as 'Theatreland'. Its history goes back to the Restoration in 1660, when indoor theatres became popular. The early ones have been rebuilt, often multiple times, but the identities of Drury Lane (1662), Haymarket (1710) and Covent Garden (1732) were continuous. Shaftesbury Avenue, a new street from the 1880s, contains 'boulevard' theatres with rich Edwardian decoration. Another cluster sits between St Martin's Lane and Charing Cross Road. The National Theatre on the South Bank belongs in another cluster with the Old and Young Vic, and the reconstructed Shakespeare's Globe beyond. Experimental and fringe theatre thrives in cheaper venues further afield. Theatreland supports costumiers and suppliers, and theatres are symbiotic with bars and restaurants for the clientele and the performers. Historically, these were often integrated, as at the Criterion, which was developed by caterers from 1870, while the Savoy Theatre (1881) was joined by its hotel under the same management. Less savoury was the sex trade that often accompanied theatres in Victorian London, either on the streets (Haymarket above all), at stage doors or in the bars of the variety theatres.

3-SECOND SURVEY
London's heart is in its theatres, even if they survive by staging many musicals-of-the-movie.

3-MINUTE OVERVIEW
London's theatres have largely survived for live performance owing to protection of their use by special planning laws, even when disused. Many are also listed buildings, and some owners, including Delfont Mackintosh (which owns eight theatres) and Andrew Lloyd-Webber (who owns six), have undertaken much-needed restorations, for example at the Palace Theatre (now sold to Nimax) and Drury Lane. The two opera houses, Covent Garden and the London Coliseum, were extended and modernized for the millennium using public funding.

RELATED TOPICS
See also
THE EAST & WEST ENDS
page 36

FILM
page 84

NELL GWYN
page 132

3-SECOND BIOGRAPHIES
DAVID GARRICK
1717–79
Supreme actor, theatre manager and raiser of theatrical tone

FRANK MATCHAM
1854–1920
Architect of London's Coliseum and Hippodrome

HUGH 'BINKIE' BEAUMONT
1908–73
Co-founder of producers H. M. Tennant, the uncrowned king of West End theatre in his time

30-SECOND TEXT
Alan Powers

London's theatres have been pulling in the crowds for many centuries.

1650
Born in Hereford, London or Oxford

1665
Begins her acting career in Bridges Street Theatre

1670
Gives birth to her first son, Charles, who becomes Earl of Burford

1664
Enters the theatre world as an orange seller

1668
Starts an affair with King Charles II

1671
Gives birth to her second son, James, who dies in Paris aged six

1671
Retires from acting

1687
Dies from complications caused by advanced syphilis

NELL GWYN

'Pretty, witty Nell', as the diarist Samuel Pepys called her, is Britain's most affectionately remembered mistress, whose rags-to-riches life story epitomized the liberalization of the Restoration era. Her good looks, endearing character, sharp wit and formidable talent projected her from an indigent childhood in the impoverished neighbourhoods around Covent Garden to the country's first female comedy actress and the mistress of King Charles II before her untimely death aged just 37.

Nell Gwyn learned acting the hard way. The assistance she gave her mother in running a bawdyhouse (brothel) and her time spent hawking goods in London's streets hardened her character and honed her prodigious social skills and sense of comic timing. The reinstatement of the theatre after its virtual prohibition during Oliver Cromwell's Protectorate and Charles II's legalization of acting for women in 1662, allowed actresses like Nell Gwyn to practise their chosen trade. Her introduction to theatre was as an orange seller in the Theatre Royal, Drury Lane, but within a year she was working as an actress. In March 1665 she performed in John Dryden's *The Indian Emperour*, playing opposite the celebrated actor Charles Hart, who became her lover. The pair performed together in numerous Restoration comedies, such as *The Maiden Queen* also by Dryden. Their popularity invited much attention.

In 1667 Gwyn began an affair with the poet and courtier, Charles Sackville (Lord Buckhurst), whom she wittily labelled 'Charles the Second', after Charles Hart, her 'Charles the First'. Within a year she was cavorting with her 'Charles the Third', the real Charles II. The relationship between the king and Nell Gwyn was well known and became the subject of numerous satires. In 1670, she gave birth to her first child, Charles, who was the king's seventh son by five mistresses. The following year she bore her second son, James, and retired from the theatre, aged just 21. Of Charles II's 13 mistresses, Nell Gwyn was the least demanding. He respected her restraint and afforded her a number of properties, including a townhouse on Pall Mall, a country house in Windsor and a summer retreat on the site of what became the popular Bagnigge Wells Spa near the banks of the River Fleet. A plaque from 1680 featuring a face and the words 'This is Bagnigge House' is retained in the wall of 61–63 King's Cross Road, and Bagnigge House and Nell Gwyn's name survive in the titles of two Islington Council housing blocks on the nearby Margery Street Estate. Nell Gwyn was buried at St Martin-in-the-Fields, in the same neighbourhood where she had spent her impecunious childhood.

Edward Denison

ENIGMATIC LONDON

ENIGMATIC LONDON
GLOSSARY

Black Death, 1348 Known at the time as the Great Pestilence, the Black Death was the most devastating pandemic ever caused by the bubonic plague, killing more than half of Europe's population and half London's population (40,000) in two years after its arrival in 1348.

bubonic plague A type of bacterial infection responsible for successive pandemics that killed millions of people worldwide from the fourteenth to seventeenth centuries.

City of London A city and county of Britain governed by the City of London Corporation covering a geographic area broadly defined by the walls of the Roman settlement, also referred to as the Square Mile.

dot map A method of surveying using data collection recorded in the form of dots on a map to represent the incidence and geographic location of a phenomenon.

grave-goods Objects buried with a corpse, usually in the form of personal possessions and artefacts or offerings believed to help the deceased in the afterlife.

Great Fire, 1666 London's largest ever fire, which started in a bakery in Pudding Lane and over the course of three days swept through the medieval streetscape, destroying more than 13,000 wooden buildings, including 87 parish churches and the old St Paul's Cathedral.

Great Plague, 1665 The last major outbreak of the bubonic plague, which killed more than 100,000 Londoners, or a quarter of the city's population.

Industrial Revolution The rise and proliferation of industrial forms of production and manufacturing over manual labour and craft production, originating in Britain in the mid-seventeenth century and quickly spreading throughout the world.

Londinium The Roman title for London, established shortly after their invasion of Britain in 43 CE, from which the modern city gains its name.

miasma Ancient theory purporting that the spread of disease was caused by noxious air caused by rotting matter, which held sway until disproved by the advance of modern science in the mid-nineteenth century.

Peasants' Revolt, 1381 Uprising among peasants of Kent and Essex that resulted in a march on London led by Wat Tyler and the unprecedented capture of the Tower of London. The young King Richard II negotiated with the peasants, though his concessions were later retracted and Tyler was killed by the Lord Mayor of London.

resurrectionist Also known as body-snatchers, resurrectionists exhumed dead bodies to sell for anatomical research, a practice that reached its peak in the eighteenth century when medical research was flourishing and the law did little to deter such activities.

GRAVEYARDS

the 30-second tour

Dating to 4000 BCE, London's earliest known burial site is located in Blackwall in the East End. Prehistoric graveyards, mainly cremation fields, have also been discovered in west London, while there is evidence that the Thames may also have been used for prehistoric burial. Roman Londinium was surrounded by graveyards, containing thousands of burials with exotic grave-goods. Medieval monasteries had extensive cemeteries, with senior clergy and wealthy patrons buried in the churches, and the poorer outside, sometimes in mass graves at times of catastrophe. Legend has it that London is covered in plague pits, but only two small Black Death cemeteries have been excavated. Increased population, urbanization and epidemics such as cholera and typhoid caused major problems. In the nineteenth century, the burial grounds choked and bodies could not fully decompose. There were notorious problems with resurrectionists robbing graves to sell bodies for anatomical study. London's graveyards were closed by Act of Parliament in 1851, yet people kept dying. One solution was to open a cemetery outside London served by special train; thus the London Necropolis Company was founded and the Brookwood Cemetery opened. London's modern cemeteries are almost full; where will the dead be buried in future?

3-SECOND SURVEY
Over the millennia, London's graveyards have gone from small islands of commemoration to elaborate landscapes devoted to the dead.

3-MINUTE OVERVIEW
In the eighteenth century concerns were raised about overflowing small parish cemeteries but it wasn't until 1832 that the first of what became known as the Magnificent Seven Cemeteries was opened to counter the problem. These are architectural masterpieces and havens of solitude from modern, hectic London, to be found at Kensal Green, Highgate, West Norwood, Abney Park, Nunhead, Brompton and Bow.

RELATED TOPICS
See also
PARKS, GARDENS &
OPEN SPACES
page 116

EPIDEMICS
page 148

3-SECOND BIOGRAPHY
MRS BASIL HOLMES
1861–unknown
Researched and published the fascinating and informative *London Burial Grounds* in 1897, describing nearly 500 sites

30-SECOND TEXT
Jane Sidell

London is a paradise for ghost hunters, abounding with hundreds of burial grounds from the small and private to the vast and public.

SUBTERRANEAN LONDON

the 30-second tour

Built on a chalky basin under

soft clay, two millennia of development mean a deep history and active infrastructure are well preserved below London. The city's rich archaeological record reveals Roman bathhouses and medieval priories below office blocks and estates. The Thames Tunnel was the world's first tunnel under a navigable river. Opened in 1843, it was the work of Marc and Isambard Kingdom Brunel, Britain's great engineering heroes. Next was the world's first underground railway, in 1863, beginning a vast transport network 6 to 56 metres (20 to 185 feet) below the ground. But perhaps the mightiest underground achievement was Joseph Bazalgette's extraordinary sewer system, opened in 1865, revolutionizing Londoners' waste. The Thames Embankments of the 1870s effectively covered Bazalgette's low-level sewer, the underground railway, telegraph services and water mains in a palimpsest of subterranean improvements. And from 1927 even the post was carried 20 metres (65 feet) underground on a driverless railway line. Underground became a place of refuge in World War II when eight deep-level air-raid shelters were constructed across London; and again when Clapham South's shelter was used to temporarily house West Indian immigrants arriving on the *Empire Windrush* in 1948.

3-SECOND SURVEY
London's extensive archaeological record, subterranean networks of Victorian improvements and twentieth-century communication systems amount to centuries of history below ground.

3-MINUTE OVERVIEW
It was the Great Stink of 1858, and awful outbreaks of cholera, that galvanized the Metropolitan Board of Works to invest in a proper sewer system. Civil engineer Joseph Bazalgette designed the ingenious network of tunnels that carried waste eastwards along gravitational outfall routes. Thanks to his foresight – constructing the tunnels twice as wide as Victorians needed – it remains the foundation for today's sewers.

RELATED TOPICS
See also
ENGINEERING
page 106

THE UNDERGROUND
page 110

EPIDEMICS
page 148

LOST RIVERS
page 150

3-SECOND BIOGRAPHY
JOSEPH BAZALGETTE
1819–91
Civil engineer who masterminded the London Victorian sewer system that still serves modern London

30-SECOND TEXT
Emily Gee

With one of the world's largest underground railway systems and hundreds of miles of Victorian sewers, there's much more to London than meets the eye!

PADDINGTON

THAMES EMBANKMENT

WHITECHAPEL

CRIME

the 30-second tour

London has a long and bloody

relationship with crime, the consequences of which have bestowed on the world such familiar names as Scotland Yard, the Old Bailey and Sherlock Holmes. Crime has shaped the city's social, physical and legal character, pioneering new forms of crime prevention, legal institutions and even literary genres. The Romans were the first to establish an organized system of crime prevention in London. In 1285 the Statute Victatis London dealt with policing, which was administered locally by paid watchmen. By the eighteenth century, the Industrial Revolution precipitated London's rapid urbanization and expansion, demanding a more effective and organized system of policing. In 1798 the Thames River Police was established and later subsumed into the newly created Metropolitan Police following the 1829 Metropolitan Police Act. Colonel Charles Rowan and Richard Mayne (from whom the policeman's moniker 'Bobbie' was derived) were placed in charge of the new force, conducting their work from 4 Whitehall Place, which backed onto a small courtyard called Great Scotland Yard, the name becoming synonymous with the Metropolitan Police Headquarters ever since. The City of London Police, established in 1832, maintained their independence from the Metropolitan Police.

3-SECOND SURVEY
London has three independent police forces: the Metropolitan Police, the City of London Police and the British Transport Police.

3-MINUTE OVERVIEW
London has hosted some of the world's most infamous criminals, from Jack the Ripper, who terrorized Victorian London, to the violent East End gangland twins, Ronald and Reginald Kray. One of London's most extraordinary crimes was the Sidney Street Siege of 1911. An impasse between police and the Latvian Gardstein gang led to the Home Secretary, Winston Churchill, sending in heavy artillery, but the gang members died before they arrived when the house burned down.

RELATED TOPICS
See also
REFUGE
page 30

PROTEST
page 92

SHERLOCK HOLMES
page 144

TORTURE & EXECUTION
page 146

3-SECOND BIOGRAPHIES
SIR CHARLES ROWAN
& SIR RICHARD MAYNE
1782–1852 & 1796–1868
Joint first Commissioners of the Metropolitan Police

GILBERT MACKENZIE TRENCH
1885–1979
Surveyor and architect for the Metropolitan Police. Designed the blue Police Box (1928) immortalized by its depiction as the Tardis in *Dr Who*

30-SECOND TEXT
Edward Denison

Crime has long held a central place in London's popular culture.

1854
Born, 6 January
(disputed)

1866
Sent to a grammar school
in Yorkshire

1872
Enters Christ Church
College, Oxford

1879
Investigates his third
case in London (now
living in Montague
Street)

1881
Meets Dr Watson and
takes residence in 221b
Baker Street

1887
Arthur Conan Doyle
publishes first of Dr
Watson's accounts
A Study in Scarlet

1891
Holmes fakes his death

1903
Retires and moves
to rural Sussex

SHERLOCK HOLMES

For many, Sherlock Holmes

remains the greatest detective of the modern age, advancing forensic science and displaying immense powers of deductive reasoning to resolve complex, sophisticated and often violent crimes.

Born in 1854 (the exact date is a matter of dispute), Holmes received a classical training, and read chemistry as an undergraduate. Finding little pleasure in the company of others, and displaying just as little interest in the pursuit of the arts or pure sciences, Holmes spent his youth refining his ability to deduce general statements from particular material evidence. He also honed his martial skills, becoming a first-class boxer, martial artist, swordsman and rifleman, as well as displaying talent as an actor. Holmes enjoyed using his skills to investigate crimes brought to him by fellow students and their parents.

Encouraged by success in these investigations Holmes moved to London in 1877 and established himself as a private detective. The first six years, while not unsuccessful, failed financially. To relieve hardship Holmes secured a lodger in his apartment at 221b Baker Street (an unassuming London street near the Metropolitan Line railway station): a Dr John H. Watson. It is Watson's published works (brought to public attention by his agent Arthur Conan Doyle) that provide knowledge of Holmes and his investigations. Perhaps too sympathetic, Watson gained intimate knowledge of the detective, but is never a wholly reliable witness.

Though able to call on a network of informants, including the 'Baker Street Irregulars', it is on his unrivalled knowledge of the geology and topography of London that Holmes relied. Holmes resolved some of the most infamous crimes in London, foiled the most notorious London criminals – including Professor Moriarty – and worked for an astonishing range of London society, from visiting princes to resident governesses. Watson's accounts of Holmes continue to excite imaginative reconstructions of late-Victorian London.

Holmes was first presumed dead in 1891, when after a fierce struggle with Moriarty at the Reichenbach Falls (Switzerland) no trace of his body was found. In fact, Holmes had survived, and returned to London in 1894. Within ten years, he retired from private detective work, becoming an apiarist in Sussex. Holmes withdrew drastically from public life and his exact date of death remains unknown. Sherlock and his elder brother Mycroft were bachelors and no family survived them.

Nick Beech

TORTURE & EXECUTION

the 30-second tour

Until the nineteenth century, public executions drew huge crowds who revelled in the spectacle of the hangman's noose. London's longest serving gallows was at Tyburn, now beneath Marble Arch. For over six centuries prisoners were paraded from Newgate Prison along the route of Oxford Street to be hanged. When Tyburn closed in 1783, Newgate erected its own gallows from which people were hanged in public until 1868 when the hanging of Fenian, Michael Barrett, marked the end of execution as public entertainment. Nearby Smithfield was a multifunctional execution ground. In 1305 William Wallace, the Scottish patriot, was hanged, disembowelled and cut into pieces there. Wat Tyler, the leader of the Peasants' Revolt, was beheaded there in 1381, and in 1410 John Badby was burned in a barrel for denying substantiation. Smithfield also hosted Britain's first public boiling, when Richard Rouse, the Bishop of Rochester's cook, was boiled to death in 1531. Other popular gallows were at Execution Dock in Wapping and Charing Cross, which also boasted a pillory for public flogging. At 2pm on 30 January 1649, Londoners observed the city's most famous execution when King Charles I was led out of a window of Banqueting House on Whitehall onto a scaffold and beheaded in one fell swoop of the executioner's axe.

Londoners used to revel in the spectacle of a public execution.

EPIDEMICS

the 30-second tour

London is a crowded city.

Proximity to others, limited hygiene facilities, easily contaminated water and a constant stream of visitors have ensured its history has been marked by disease, epidemic and plague. Fear of disease shaped its social patterns, with the rich fleeing the city for the countryside, and poorer areas being feared as sites of infection. The Black Death of 1348 and the Great Plague of 1665 are the most notorious of over 40 outbreaks of the bubonic plague, which not only spread terror, but also posed civic authorities practical challenges such as how to dispose of the dead or how to alert the authorities to infection. Poor sanitary conditions aided major outbreaks of typhoid, typhus and cholera in the nineteenth century, which then helped to generate a fear of the poor and of immigrants (who were believed to carry disease) and support belief in disease-spreading miasmas, as well as inspiring the first serious attempts to map and mitigate such challenges to public health. Echoes of such past epidemics remain in the fabric of the city, such as the discovery of plague pits under construction sites, while modern epidemics, such as HIV/AIDS and the rise of drug-resistant tuberculosis, continue to trouble public health authorities.

3-SECOND SURVEY
London's population has always been troubled by epidemics, creating cultural repercussions as well as posing a threat to life itself.

3-MINUTE OVERVIEW
In 1854, Dr John Snow famously removed the handle of the water pump in Broad Street in modern-day Soho, thereby halting a cholera epidemic. Although recent research suggests that the epidemic was already waning before Snow's action, and that he did not use a 'dot map' to locate the source of the disease, he has entered the history books as a heroic example of the success of a scientific approach to public health and disease.

RELATED TOPICS
See also
THE EAST & WEST ENDS
page 36

IMPROVEMENTS
page 50

GRAVEYARDS
page 138

3-SECOND BIOGRAPHY
DR JOHN SNOW
1813—1858
Physician and pioneer epidemiologist, who was sceptical of the miasma theory of disease and instead blamed the transmission of cholera on contaminated water

30-SECOND TEXT
Matthew Shaw

London's history is beset by epidemics of one form or another, the worst of which culled up to half of the city's population.

MEMENTO MORI

LOST RIVERS

the 30-second tour

The River Thames might be the largest and most famous waterway in London, but it has never been alone in draining the region's water, whether it has fallen from the sky, risen from springs or been flushed from our homes. The area around London was once laced with over 20 rivers winding their way to the Thames, but today nearly all have been buried beneath the vast metropolis, channelled into culverts, pipes and sewers. Hidden from view, these tributaries have left an indelible mark on the city's physical, etymological, literary and political landscapes. Echoes of the small brook that ran through the Roman wall reverberate in the conjoined name of Walbrook in the City of London. The annular form of the Oval is a fossilized relic of the Effra's once meandering course. The Fleet's stinking condition by the nineteenth century inspired local resident, Charles Dickens, to make it the setting for Fagin's lair in *Oliver Twist*. London's Royal Parks were furnished with lakes created by diverting rivers such as the Westbourne, which filled Hyde Park's Serpentine. London's rivers have left their mark on the political map too, with these ancient obstacles forming boundaries that continue to separate local authorities – the Fleet divides Camden and Islington just as the Westbourne separates Westminster from Kensington and Chelsea.

3-SECOND SURVEY
London sits in a geological basin that was once awash with small rivers that ran like veins into the main artery of the Thames.

3-MINUTE OVERVIEW
London's largest lost river was the Fleet, which flowed from Hampstead Heath through Camden Town to the Thames, where it was once nearly 200 metres (650 feet) wide and where Christopher Wren proposed Venetian-style embankments. Swimmers would frequent this brook around St Pancras, but by the nineteenth century it had deteriorated severely. The foul-smelling ditch was covered and today it is a sewer beneath Farringdon Road, though its ancient course is evidenced in the steep slopes around Clerkenwell and Holborn Viaduct.

RELATED TOPICS
See also
GEOLOGY & GEOGRAPHY
page 16

THE THAMES
page 22

SUBTERRANEAN LONDON
page 140

3-SECOND BIOGRAPHIES
CHRISTOPHER WREN
1632–1723
Architect who supervised major improvements to the Fleet in the late seventeenth century

CHARLES DICKENS
1812–70
Lived near the banks of the Fleet and was inspired by the impoverished setting created by this once proud river

30-SECOND TEXT
Edward Denison

London's submerged rivers are remembered in place names, topography, street patterns and political boundaries.

MAPPING LONDON

the 30-second tour

3-SECOND SURVEY
London was first mapped as a city in the sixteenth century and has been captured in beautiful, harrowing and useful maps through the centuries.

3-MINUTE OVERVIEW
In the 1890s, the reformer and social researcher, Charles Booth, set out to record the wealth and poverty of Londoners in an extraordinarily detailed map: *Life and Labour of the People in London*. His army of researchers went door-to-door recording residents' work and incomes and colour-coding these in seven bands from the 'Lowest class. Vicious, semi-criminal' (black) to 'Upper-middle and Upper classes. Wealthy' (yellow). Pockets of black and dark blue next to swathes of yellow and red illustrate how intermingled late Victorian London was.

London has been pictorially recorded since the first maps of the city as a whole emerged in the 1550s. The artists Wyngaerde and Hollar meticulously captured the layout and topography of late medieval Westminster, the City of London and Southwark in their panoramas of 1543 and 1647. These Renaissance depictions would have been an utter revelation for contemporary Londoners. Maps were more widely used following the Great Fire, such as in 1677 when John Leake recorded the remaining buildings and the zone of devastation. This would be repeated three centuries later during World War II when the government collated information gathered by air-raid wardens to map the degree of loss to London's buildings and, by correlation, human life. Equally unsettling, yet useful to historians, are Charles Booth's maps from the 1890s, which also used colour to map London's social classes. Colour was introduced again in Harry Beck's map of 1931, which made a design triumph of the London Underground system and became the model for underground railway maps around the world. Around this time, Phyllis Pearsall began her epic journey to capture every road in London in the best-known street atlas: the trusty *A-Z*, which has assisted motorists and pedestrians alike ever since.

RELATED TOPICS
See also
FIRE!
page 44

THE UNDERGROUND
page 110

3-SECOND BIOGRAPHIES
ANTON VAN DEN WYNGAERDE & WENCESLAUS HOLLAR
1525–71 & 1607–77
Artists who created the first panoramas of London

CHARLES BOOTH
1840–1916
Mapped the economic reality of late Victorian London in graphic colour

HARRY BECK
1902–74
Designed London Underground's iconic map

PHYLLIS PEARSALL
1906–96
Created London's street atlas, the *A-Z*

30-SECOND TEXT
Emily Gee

People have tried to make sense of London by mapping its myriad features.

RESOURCES

BOOKS

*The Fields Beneath: The History of
One London Village*
Gillian Tindall
(Eland, 2010)

Georgian London
John Summerson
(Yale University Press, 2003)

A Guide to the Architecture of London
Edward Jones and Christopher Woodward
(Phoenix, 2013)

*Lived in London: Blue Plaques and
the Stories Behind Them*
Emily Cole
(Yale University Press, 2009)

London: A Life in Maps
Peter Whitfield
(British Library, 2006)

London: A Social History
Roy Porter
(Penguin, 2000)

The London Encyclopaedia
Christopher Hibbert, Ben Weinreb,
John Keay and Julia Keay
(Macmillan, 2008)

London Suburbs
Andrew Saint, et al.
(Merrell Holberton, 1999)

London: The Biography
Peter Ackroyd
(Vintage, 2001)

*London's Archaeological Secrets:
A World City Revealed*
Chris Thomas
(Yale University Press, 2003)

London's Cemeteries
Darren Beach
(Metro Publications, 2011)

New London Architecture
Kenneth Powell
(Merrell, 2005)

*Outcast London: A study in the relationship
between classes in Victorian society*
Gareth Stedman Jones
(Verso, 2013)

*Played in London – Charting the Heritage
of a City at Play*
Simon Inglis
(English Heritage, 2014)

The Pleasures of London
Felix Barker and Peter Jackson
(London Topographical Society, 2008)

Religion in Medieval London
Bruno Barber, Christopher Thomas
and Bruce Watson
(Museum of London Archaeology, 2013)

A Revolution in London Housing:
LCC Housing Architects and their Work
1893–1914
Susan Beattie
(The Architectural Press, 1980)

The Small House in Eighteenth-Century
London: A Social and Architectural History
Peter Guillery
(Yale University Press, 2004)

The Survey of London
John Stow
(The History Press, 2005)

WEBSITES

British History Online
www.british-history.ac.uk/catalogue/london

The British Monarchy
www.royal.gov.uk

Dennis Severs' House
www.dennissevershouse.co.uk

London Architecture
www.londonarchitecture.co.uk

London Parks & Gardens Trust
www.londongardenstrust.org

London Transport Museum
www.ltmuseum.co.uk

Londonist
londonist.com

The Museum of London
www.museumoflondon.org.uk

Spitalfields Life
spitalfieldslife.com

UK Parliament
www.parliament.uk

NOTES ON CONTRIBUTORS

EDITOR

Dr Edward Denison is an architectural historian, writer and photographer. Over the last two decades he has worked as an independent consultant and more recently as an academic specializing in modern architectural history. He is a Research Associate and Lecturer at The Bartlett School of Architecture (UCL) and has published many works including: *Ultra-Modernism – Architecture and Modernity in Manchuria* (HKUP, 2016); *Luke Him Sau: Architect – China's Missing Modern* (Wiley, 2014); *30-Second Architecture* (Ivy Press, 2013); *The Life of the British Home: An Architectural History* (Wiley, 2012); *McMorran & Whitby* (RIBA, 2009); *Modernism in China – Architectural Visions and Revolutions* (Wiley, 2008); *Building Shanghai – The Story of China's Gateway* (Wiley, 2006); *Asmara – Africa's Secret Modernist City* (Merrell, 2003).

CONTRIBUTORS

Nick Beech is Lecturer in the History of London at Queen Mary University of London. He lives by Bedford Park, the first garden suburb in the west of London, and travels every day by the District Line to the People's Palace on Mile End Road, in the east.

Emily Gee was born in north London and lives in Camden Town, not far from the now-covered Fleet River and within the parish of Old St Pancras. An architectural historian, she has worked in listing at Historic England (formerly English Heritage) since 2001 and is Head of Designation, helping to recognize and protect London's most special buildings and sites. Emily also teaches London's architectural history and is a council member of the Camden History Society. Her special subject is housing for women in Victorian and Edwardian London.

Simon Inglis is a writer on the heritage of sport and recreation. He has written a number of bestselling books on stadiums, including the *Football Grounds of Britain*, voted by the *Guardian* as the best sports book of the twentieth century. The *Daily Telegraph* described him as 'a national treasure who should be encouraged at all costs'. Since 2004 he has edited the English Heritage series *Played in Britain*. Published as part of that series in 2014, his latest book is *Played in London – Charting the Heritage of a City at Play*.

Alan Powers grew up in London and only left temporarily to study at Cambridge. He is a historian, curator and teacher, specializing in twentieth-century British art, architecture and design. He has had a long association with the conservation charity, the Twentieth Century Society, which pioneered the care of buildings after 1914. He is an editor of its academic journal, *Twentieth Century Architecture*, and its series of monographs, *Twentieth Century Architects*.

Matthew Shaw is the Librarian of the Institute of Historical Research, and formerly a curator at the British Library. He is the author of *Historic Lives: the Duke of Wellington* and *Time and the French Revolution: A History of the French Republican Calendar* and the photographer for the collaboration, *Stoller's Départ*, a tale of a convoluted bicycle ride from the British Museum to the British Library.

Jane Sidell is an archaeologist who has rummaged around in London for all her working life, first at the Museum of London and then at English Heritage/Historic England, where she is currently Inspector of Ancient Monuments. Her passions lie with the history and natural history of the Thames, and how past Londoners have tamed and used the river, which is a subject she has written on extensively. She is equally passionate about enthusing and informing Londoners about their past.

INDEX

ACKNOWLEDGMENTS

PICTURE CREDITS
The publisher would like to thank the following for permission to reproduce copyright material:

Alamy Stock Photo/WENN Ltd: 85.
Biodiversity Heritage Library: 105.
Bridgeman Images/Private Collection/The Stapleton Collection: 87.
Clipart.com: 125, 143.
Flickr/British Library: 29, 39, 79, 99, 109, 117, 129, 131, 147; Tom Bastin: 51; Steve Cadman: 69; David Holt: 139; National Archives: 93; Paul Wilkinson: 127.
Getty Images/Davies/Stringer: 71; Erica Echenberg: 91; Francis Partridge: 87; George C. Beresford/Stringer: 87; Heritage Images: 67, 69, 87, 147; Keystone-France: 31; Popperfoto: 69; Print Collector: 93; Science & Society Picture Library: 109; Terry Disney/Stringer: 143; Ullstein Bild: 141.
Les Misérables artwork © Cameron Mackintosh (Overseas) Limited 1985–2016; Les Misérables ® Cameron Mackintosh (Overseas) Limited 1998–2016: 37.
Library of Congress, Washington DC: 29, 82, 85, 93, 109, 123, 132, 141, 147.
National Gallery of Art, Washington: 81.
New York Public Library: 37, 87, 131.
Rex/Shutterstock/Elisa Leonelli: 91 (Design © Vivienne Westwood), Sheila Rock: 91, Richard Young: 91.
Shutterstock/A C Manley: 121; akiyoko: 123; aleks-p: 123; Aleksandar Todorovic: 61; Aleksandra H. Kossowska: 2; Alessandro Colle: 117; Alexander Raths: 121; Andreas R: 39; Andy Lidstone: 7; aperturesound: 129; ar3ding: 27; arturasker: 117; Ball Songwut: 151; Baloncici: 151; BasPhoto: 37, 47; Bata Zivanovic: 131; Bikeworldtravel: 37, 111, 119; Boltenkoff: 121; Chris Jenner: 23, 89; chrisdorney: 37, 42, 153; Claudio Divizia: 19, 20, 67, 71, 103; ConstantinosZ: 85; David Fowler: 93; Denis Makarenko: 85; Dutourdumonde Photography: 39; Elena Rostunova: 93; elenaburn: 129; elesi: 9; Eric Isselee: 69; Erni: 107; Everett Historical: 31, 37, 45, 59; Evikka: 31; filmlandscape: 41; FooT Too: 31; fractalgr: 27; Georgios Kollidas: 61, 62; grafvision: 51; grynold: 39; Hein Nouwens: 17, 27; Holly Kuchera: 51; homydesign: 87; I R Stone: 37, 123; Iakov Filimonov: 103; irin-k: 117; Jacek Wojnarowski: 49; Jacqueline Abromeit: 139; jan kranendock: 29; jaroslava V: 25; jennyt: 85; Jiri Flogel: 31; Justin Black: 25; Kichigin: 143; Kiev.Victor: 37, 41, 51, 65, 71, 73, 105, 129; Ksenia Palimski: 19; Lance Bellers: 131; Luciano Mortula: 123; lynea: 17, 37; majeczka: 67, 125; Maks Narodenko: 85; Maria Arts: 103; Marzolino: 17; mayakova: 91; Milos Luzanin: 153; Mitch Gunn: 125; monticello: 123; Mordechai Meiri: 31; Morphart Creation: 23, 25, 27, 53; Nick_Nick: 31; nicku: 17, 89; nui7711: 89; Oleksiy Mark: 53; Pan_Da: 45; pcruciatti: 7; peresanz: 143; Peter Lorimer: 47; Petra Mezei: 139; Philip Bird LRPS CPAGB: 121; PHILIPIMAGE: 85; Photo Balance: 125; Photo House: 89; pio3: 73; QQ7: 23; Ray_of_Light: 10–11; Rob Wilson: 125; Ron Ellis: 29; Rosa Jay: 149; Rui Saraiva: 107; Ruslan Kudrin: 87; Sellmepixels: 49; sematadesign: 37; Songquan Deng: 7; Steve Baker: 111; STILLFX: 71; Studio DMM Photography, Designs & Art: 39; SvedOliver: 151; Tadeusz Ibrom: 73; Taviphoto: 103; Timurpix: 31; Triff: 153; Tupungato: 85; unlit: 123; Viacheslav Lopatin: 19; Vittorio Caramazza: 59; Wallpaper fabric swatches: 79; YANGCHAO: 119; Yuriy Mykhaylov: 23.
The Tube map has been reproduced with the kind permission of Transport for London: 153.
The University of Texas at Austin: 19.
Walters Art Museum: 25.
Wellcome Library, London: 17, 19, 23, 25, 27, 37, 39, 41, 51, 53, 61, 65, 99, 100, 103, 105, 107, 119, 141, 143, 147, 149, 151, 153.
Wikimedia Commons/Siddharth Krish: 144.
Yale Center for British Art: 45, 47, 49, 59, 61, 65, 79, 81, 99, 105, 117, 119, 125, 127, 131.